Up Mount Everest Without a Paddle

Derek Nimmo

Up Mount Everest Without a Paddle

Robson Books

First published in Great Britain in 1988 by Robson Books Ltd,
Bolsover House, 5–6 Clipstone Street, London W1P 7EB.

British Library Cataloguing in Publication Data

Nimmo, Derek
  Up Mount Everest without a paddle.
  I. Title
  828'.91409

ISBN 0-86051-549-4

Typeset by Rowland Phototypesetting Ltd,
Bury St Edmunds, Suffolk

Printed in Great Britain by St Edmundsbury Press Ltd,
Bury St Edmunds, Suffolk

To my mother,
who made everything happen

Contents

Introduction

THIRTY YEARS AGO, the life of an English actor was very different from that enjoyed today. However successful, he would have spent a great deal of the year touring the English provinces. Travelling by train; always on a Sunday, when it was said that only actors and fish travelled on that day. Greetings to friends at Crewe Junction; living in fairly nasty digs, or, if topping the bill, in indifferent hotels was his cheerless lot. Today, thanks to television, new markets for the actor's talents have appeared all over the world. Because of this, a chum of mine created a theatre export business. For the last twelve years now I have worked for him. We put on plays on a regular basis, all over the world – from Bermuda to Bangkok; Amman to Athens; Singapore to Sydney; some twenty-eight countries in all.

As you can imagine, acting in plays in somewhere like Abu Dhabi is very different from appearing in the West End of London. In London these days one is lucky if thirty per cent of the audience speak English as their first language. In the United Arab Emirates, ninety-eight per cent of your audience *are* English.

One has, of course, to be fairly careful with the plays that one selects. In Papua New Guinea, for instance, it would be tolerably foolhardy to put on *One For the Pot* and even more dangerous, perhaps, to risk a production of *There's a Girl in My Soup*. Next year we are starting in Beijing – perhaps with *No Sex Please We're British*. This would probably be a curiously satisfying play to present in the People's Republic of China as hitherto, I suspect, they have always thought that lust is something that affects Chinese motorcars.

Putting on plays in so many places means that I spend at least six months of the year abroad. Sometimes, several weeks of the year when added together, on an aeroplane. In this little book, I have endeavoured to put down some of my own favourite travel stories together with some of the curious things that have happened to me as I perambulate around the world. The name our actors tend to give the production company is 'The Jet Set Rep' and as we present mainly comedies, laughter is a fairly happy export trade with which to be involved. It's certainly much nicer than the business of a man I was talking to over dinner in Dubai the other day. He had quizzed me about our touring theatre and then I asked him what he did. 'I'm a population controller,' he replied.

When he had gone, I turned to a friend who was still at the dining-table. 'What did he mean?' I asked.

'Oh,' he said, 'he's an arms dealer selling weapons to Iran!'

No, I think laughter is much more likely to produce peace than weaponry. Perhaps, having finished this book, you will agree.

Innocents Abroad

SEVERAL SUMMERS AGO in Corfu, on one abandoned night, I consumed what can only be described as a satisfaction of Retsina. Now Retsina is not everyone's cup of tea – or even glass of wine, come to think of it – but perversely enough I have a considerable affection for the taste of elderly turpentine. Not only is it the cup that cheers but it does tend to make me more than usually chatty and willing to listen to others and their battles against life's little difficulties. On this particular evening, my wife would have me believe, fortified by the wine, I found myself involved in such a conversation. My new-found companion, it seemed, had a problem of some moment, namely a very large brass four-poster bed. This he wished to dispose of as funds were urgently needed to support his wife, children, grandchildren and sundry dependent relatives. Well gosh, faced with such a worthy cause, one could hardly refuse, could one?

I am not certain how much I paid for it, but at the time it seemed as well as being an act of commendable charity a frightfully useful acquisition to boot.

Come the dawn I wasn't quite so sure – and I had to confess to myself, between aspirin tablets, that it wasn't of necessity the most sensible purchase of a lifetime.

The question was what to do with it. It really was the most enormous piece of brassware. The original recipient of the instruction 'pick up thy bed and walk' must have been dealing with a somewhat lighter model. There was obviously no way I could take it home to London (even if I had wanted to, which I didn't), but fortunately, it being on castors, I managed to push it through the village in search of a sanctuary. Eventually this was found in the shape of an old stable belonging to a Greek chum of mine. He kindly said I could leave it there until I could find it a home.

I didn't visit Corfu again until three springs later and I cannot pretend that the bed had been exactly in the forefront of my mind in the intervening years. However, finding myself back once more in the same little taverna, grinning faces reminded me of the night of the long bed. Furthermore I found that it was still lying waiting for me in Spiro's stable.

Would I be taking it home with me this time, and if so would I like to buy another one to take with it?

'No, I would not,' I said sharply.

And then disarmed by their laughter I ordered another bottle of Retsina.

Spring in Corfu is an enchanting time. There are wild flowers in such profusion that it looks as if some divine hand has thrown a vast seed packet over the island. Everybody is preparing for Easter. Houses are whitewashed; new dresses are made; and everything is newly scrubbed and gleaming. There is a feeling of mounting excitement as the great feast draws nigh. Saint Spiridon himself is brought out of his church on Palm Sunday and is trooped around the town accompanied by stiff-backed soldiers, old priests, dozens of marching bands, and scores of children carrying crosses of woven palms. Then on Easter Eve at midnight in the shadow of the great Venetian citadel the Bishop lights a candle from which all the faithful light their own candles until the whole square is ablaze with light. The bells ring out, cannons roar and people return home greeting each other on the way with the words 'Christ is risen' to the traditional feast of the new-born lamb.

That year it seemed more difficult than usual to leave that gentle island and return to the realities of the sinking pound and general economic despondency.

Standing in the queue at the departure gate I glanced around for the last time at the dreaming mountains punctuated by the pointing fingers of the cypress trees. In the distance lay sleepy villages with the white campaniles of the churches above the warm red of the tile roofs nestling beneath them. 'Oh gosh,' I thought, 'how perfect the sheer tranquillity of it . . .' My thoughts stopped abruptly. Something caught my eye that caused my heart to sink. Trundling across the tarmac towards my aircraft was a very old shooting brake and strapped to its roof in a dismantled state was the dreaded bed. There was nothing I could do about it. I just had to stand there helplessly whilst Spiro, roaring with laughter, distributed drachmas in appropriate directions which caused the awful bed to disappear into the bowels of the aeroplane. With a cheery wave Spiro was gone.

I next saw the bed in the luggage reclaim area at Gatwick – huge, brass and foreboding. There is an awfully nice little porter who has often assisted me at the airport. I again enlisted his aid. He looked outwardly unperturbed and seemed to take the bed in his tiny stride.

My wife, however, overheard him whispering to a colleague, 'That Derek Nimmo's very eccentric, you know. Always comes back with something different. This time he's brought back a bloody Spanish bed!'

The only comfort I can take from this, if comfort is the word, is the knowledge that I'm not alone in having bed problems on holiday. It seems that over-enthusiastic honeymooners have been responsible for a impressive tally of buckled legs and battered bedsprings in holiday hotels from the Costa Brava to Cleethorpes. One Scots couple managed to wreck four beds in their frenzied fortnight in Spain, and a Devon hotelier who ran a season of cut-price honeymoons paid the price to the tune of several hundred pounds after every bed in his fourteen-room hotel succumbed to his guests' amorous athletics.

Perhaps he would have been better off with a couple of newlyweds who returned home early from their honeymoon complaining that there was nothing to do in the cottage they had rented. In the absence of a television set all that they could do, according to the twenty-year-old husband, was 'eat and sleep'.

Their marriage must have been very different from that of another young couple who were covered in confusion when an elderly relative, hearing that they had some distance to drive after leaving the reception, asked, 'Are you going all the way tonight?'

Honeymoons can offer the unexpected in more than one respect. From the French Indian Ocean island of Réunion comes the tale of a young groom who went for a stroll in the moonlight with his bride. Sensing a rising call of nature, he hopped over a fence to relieve himself and dropped into a volcano – tragic proof that love really is blind.

Dropping in, if you'll forgive the pun, plagued the young couple who had, maybe a little rashly, borrowed the house in Rome belonging to Gerald Tyrwhitt-Wilson, the fourteenth Baron Berners who features elsewhere with his railway antics. Ever fond of a practical joke, Berners had made a collection of visiting cards from all the most boring people in London. These he entrusted to his butler in Rome, with the instruction that he was to deliver them at regular intervals to the young lovers during their stay in his house.

Their anxiety mounted with the steadily increasing pile of cards and they spent most of their honeymoon furtively moving about the Eternal City, terrified they were going to bump into one of their 'visitors'.

Coping with bores has always been one of the more exacting sides of travel. T. E. Lawrence attended a cocktail party in Egypt on a blistering hot day; not a gathering in which he felt entirely at home. Sipping a glass of squash, he saw approaching an English lady of uncertain years who had the reputation for fêting the great and famous. 'Ninety-two today, Colonel Lawrence. Ninety-two,' she remarked.

'Many happy returns, madam,' replied the Lord of the Desert.

He might have been in a more receptive frame of mind if he had allowed himself to indulge in one of the slightly jollier concoctions being handed round. But Lawrence was teetotal, a disposition that somehow seems at odds with travel abroad.

Ironically, it was through the temperance movement that tourism on a large scale came into being. The redoubtable Thomas Cook, a publisher and printer of temperance tracts in Leicester, began organizing cheap railway outings to

temperance galas in the early 1840s. In 1845 he organized
the first forerunner of the modern 'package' holiday. This
offered the difficult choice between four days at one of seven
recommended temperance hotels in Liverpool, or a night
there and three tempting days in merry Caernarvon, where
Cook was able to find only one man who could speak English.

The following year 350 Thomas Cook holiday-makers
headed north of the border for five days in Glasgow, Edinburgh and the Border Country. A brass band met them at
the station in Glasgow and escorted them through the city
to the Town Hall where they were regaled with a succession
of 'improving' addresses, one of which bore the riotous title
'The Natural, Moral and Political Effects of Temperance'.
That could certainly rate as a once-in-a-lifetime holiday.

Those early days of Cook's Tours were recalled in 1972
when an unprecedented offer appeared in *The Times* of 1
April, which announced that Thomas Cook and Son had
decided to offer a thousand world tours at 1872 prices. When
Cook's offices opened for business throughout the country
they were inundated with bargain hunters eager to snap up
the £210 holidays. No one in the company knew anything
about the special offer and their senior management con-
tacted *The Times* to find out what they knew about it. Not
long after, the paper's travel correspondent found himself
with a one-way ticket out of a job.

Luckily for him his colleagues rallied round and convinced
the men at the top that he'd only written a harmless April
fool to amuse them. It was a complete accident, they explained, that it had passed right through the editorial mill
and appeared in print.

Five years later the *Guardian* went to print with a seven-
page supplement on the small Third World country of San
Seriffe. This contained the familiar selection of bland articles
on the tiny nation's history, economy and tourism, carefully
edited to make sure they contained nothing that might offend
the leading British and multinational companies that had
paid for the lucrative advertisements that adorned every
page.

The first page carried pictures of the head of state, General M. J. Pica, oil drilling-rigs and sun-drenched beaches, which conveyed the pretty accurate message that San Seriffe was another oil-rich dictatorship where you could make a fast buck. 'The ten years of independence which San Seriffe celebrates today,' ran the leading article, 'have been a period of economic expansion and social development unrivalled by any other new nation.' A little further on the writer had to confess diplomatically that 'Rapid growth brings its own problems, not all of which can be solved in total composure.'

Inside the supplement the consequences of this absence of 'composure' were hinted at in other photographs. The leader of the official opposition was pictured as a broken, decrepit old man, wrapped in a blanket and clutching the handrail as he mounted that stairs in the parliament building. Another photograph showed part of what the caption described as 'General Pica's surprisingly large air force', again referred too with great tact as 'a source of comfort in a potentially difficult area of operation'.

The history of San Seriffe was featured in a fascinating article, complete with a map showing the two principal islands Caissa Superiore (Upper Case) and Caissa Inferiore (Lower Case). Alongside was a picture of an ancient stone slab inscribed with an incomprehensible script, identified as Ki-flong, which, according to the writer, 'describes "a great journey towards the sunrise".'

This, he went on to assert, 'almost certainly refers to the slow easterly movement of the islands across the oceans,' as demonstrated by the similarity of variants of the ancient script discovered in Guatemala, which apparently showed, 'that the territory may have been located off the coast of Brazil. The subsequent movement must then have been round the Cape of Good Hope.'

The advertisements included an invitation from Texaco to win a quiz and spend a fortnight in San Seriffe as the guest of racing driver James Hunt. The only snag was that the small print showed that the quiz had closed on 31 March, the day before the supplement appeared. The manufacturers of Cricket lighters placed an ad in franglais. The Perpetua University of San Seriffe offered the post of Reader in Lunar Spectroscopy to anyone with experience in extracting energy from moonbeams and able, in the words of the advertisement, to send in an application 'accompanied by a suitable consideration'.

Sunseekers weren't forgotten either. There was a inviting picture of a palm-fringed beach which only lost a little of its glamour when you read the caption 'One of the many beaches from which terrorism has been virtually eliminated.'

The advertisement that was boldest in alerting readers to this elaborate hoax was that placed by the purveyors of a popular table wine. Below a miniature of the cover page of the San Seriffe supplement ran the caption, 'It's about as likely as a duff bottle of Hirondelle.'

Anyone searching for other clues would have found them dotted all through the supplement; the most obvious giveaway being the names, including that of the island republic itself. These were all terms used in the printing trade.

It always seems a great pity when people don't enter into the spirit of innocent fun like this. A Bristol couple holidaying in Torquay treated themselves to a cabaret in one of the town's hotels one evening, during which they won first prize in a competition.

As they were presented with their bottle of champagne by the jovial compère, he told them lightheartedly, 'And you've also won a free week's holiday . . . at our new hotel in Vietnam. It's five star and you can see three of them through the roof.'

Some time later the hotel manager received a letter from a Bristol solicitor requesting that the holiday promise be honoured.

I took my family for a holiday in Vietnam, just before the Tet offensive. My wife maintains that the only reason I decided on a vacation in Saigon was so that I could send my mother-in-law pictures of bombs exploding, tanks advancing and parachutes descending. We stayed at the Caravel Hotel and there was something peculiarly decadent about sitting on the balcony at night with a glass of champagne in hand and watching the gunfire in the outer suburbs.

Our departure was somewhat delayed owing to the fact that the Viet Cong had cut off Highway One. When, however, it was proclaimed that all was safe I popped into a bank with my Barclaycard and withdrew the precise amount of Vietnamese money required for the taxi fare to the airport. My wife and I, together with the children and a mountain of luggage, climbed into the cab and off we drove.

Halfway to the airport, in what appeared to be fairly unfriendly country, the taxi driver stopped and demanded extra money before he would take us on our way. This I did not have.

Fortunately for me an American half-track came past at that point and I flagged it down. 'Excuse me, my dear fellow,' I enquired, 'do you speak English?'

'I certainly do,' replied a rather large black man sitting behind a machine-gun.

I explained my problem.

'Just leave it to me, sir,' said the soldier. He got down from his vehicle, instructed our taxi-driver to follow and climbing into the cab with a revolver in one hand ordered him to take us to the airport.

Thanks to his initiative the fare surcharge was waived.

Mystery tours aren't all they're made out to be sometimes. One year a Norwich man on holiday with his wife at Southend went on a 'mystery coach trip' and ended up back home in Norwich. They had to spend the rest of the day in the cattle market to avoid meeting friends, before catching the coach back to Southend in the evening.

Another East Anglia man who literally fell among friends was a chap from Cambridge who had to be carried back on the coach decidedly the worse for wear by his chums after a works outing to Great Yarmouth. Back in Cambridge they took him home and tucked him up in bed. He woke up in the morning with a shocking head and completely bewildered to be at home because he hadn't been on the outing at all. He was in the middle of a fortnight's holiday at Yarmouth and just happened to come across his workmates by chance. In the meantime his wife had reported him missing to the police.

Even more bizarre was the experience of Mr Nicholas Scotti of San Franscisco, but formerly from Rome, as they say Stateside, Italy. In spite of having lived in California for years, he remained close to his old roots and had acquired very little English. In 1977 he decided to visit his relatives and boarded a plane bound for his homeland. On the way the plane touched down at Kennedy Airport to refuel. Assuming that his journey was over, Mr Scotti left the plane and spent the next two days in New York convinced that he was in Rome, but having difficulty in finding his bearings.

His family had warned him of the Rome traffic, so he wasn't surprised by the heavily congested streets, or the fact that no one had been at the airport to meet him; he just assumed they'd got stuck in a jam on the way.

Setting out to find their address he wandered the streets of Manhattan marvelling at the towering buildings, but slightly surprised that the authorities had sanctioned such a wholesale demolition of all the ancient landmarks he remembered from his youth.

There also seemed to be a remarkable number of Americans visiting 'Rome', but he knew it was a popular destination for tourists and concluded that the great many signs written in English were also for their benefit.

However, there were also lots of Italian speakers who helped him on his way. One was a policeman born in Naples, who obligingly directed Mr Scotti to the bus station in fluent Italian.

He spent the next twelve hours on that bus before the driver finally turned him over to a second policeman in desperation. This one didn't speak Italian, and a slight altercation ensued as Mr Scotti expressed his amazement that a policeman in Rome couldn't even speak his native language. It was then gently explained to him that he was actually in New York.

This he flatly refused to believe. Even in the police car

that raced him out to Kennedy again with the siren wailing he stuck to his conviction. 'I know I'm in Italy,' he told an interpreter. 'This is the way they drive.'

Seeing the Sights

SIGHTSEEING HAS NEVER been all that it's been cracked up to be.

Socrates knew this 2,500 years ago and told us as much, 'See one promontory, one mountain, one sea, one river and see all.' But still we troop round, dutifully ticking off famous landmarks and monuments of great historic moment, with more than the occasional recall of that line Shelley wrote on the subject of sightseeing 'Look on my works, ye mighty, and despair.'

One feels a certain empathy with the little girl who returned from her first holiday abroad, a fortnight in Brittany, and confided to a friend, 'It was lovely, but I did get tired of being interested in everything.'

As you get older and travelwise the veneer of enthusiasm can wear pretty thin, especially when you're treated to someone else's travel saga. Beau Brummell, who had a fine line in retort when he put his mind to it, was unwillingly treated to a tedious account of a tour of the North of England made by a notoriously dull visitor. After rambling on interminably about the Dales and the Moors he could see Brummell's attention wandering and tried to draw him into the discussion by asking which of the Lakes he preferred. Turning to his valet, Brummell asked, 'Robinson, which of the Lakes do I admire?'

'Windermere, sir.'

'Windermere,' said Brummell to his visitor. 'So it is, Windermere.'

Evelyn Waugh and Harold Acton, on an ill-fated tour of southern Italy, received a rather better intentioned visit from the British consul in Naples, though neither traveller was in a mood to appreciate this courtesy. In spite of the consul's best endeavours at small talk the conversation waned and in an effort to prevent it from flagging completely he remarked brightly, 'I have a map of Mount Ararat, which I think might interest you.'

'Why should it?' asked Waugh. 'Has the Ark been found?'

When Laurence Olivier paid a visit to Noël Coward in Jamaica, his old friend suggested they visit a particular mountaintop to enjoy Coward's favourite view. The summit gained, they stood together gazing over the terraces of rain forest stretching away below. 'It looks like rows and rows of empty seats,' commented Olivier.

The last time I saw Noël Coward was when I was playing in the musical *Charlie Girl* at the Adelphi Theatre in London. Noël came round to my dressing-room after the performance, having just returned to England from a rejuvenating clinic in Switzerland. The treatment apparently required the consumption of sheep glands and Noël's secretary, Cole Lesley, told me that when the Master arrived he looked up at the hillside and espied a great flock of white sheep. Amongst the flock there was one black one. 'Ah,' said Noël, 'I see they're expecting Paul Robeson.'

Travel doesn't always broaden the mind – even when it comes at a knock-down price. A good thirty years ago British Railways devised a week-end, all-in excursion around the Hebrides, offering a forty-hour return trip by train and steamer – and all for a fiver. Three hundred people signed up for the trip from Euston, but at least one returned less than impressed by her 1,300-mile journey to the gentle isles and complaining, 'There's nothing but scenery up there.'

In 1825 Dr William Buckland, geologist, palaeontologist and twenty years later Dean of Westminster, spent his honeymoon in Sicily and treated himself and his bride to a day out visiting the relics of Santa Rosalia lovingly housed in the church built in her honour on Monte Pellegrino.

The new Mrs Buckland obediently followed her husband's enthusiasm for old bones and frequently the organic matter that once surrounded them. (Not only did Buckland pinch Ben Jonson's heel bone from Westminster Abbey, he also tucked into Louis XIV's embalmed heart at dinner one evening and was frequently sampling gastronomic delights as varied as mole and alligator.) So together, they ascended to the spot where the bones of the young saint had been found surrounded in a case of lime a couple of centuries earlier.

The relics were proudly displayed to the great scholar by their guardians, who clearly hadn't bargained on Buckland's anatomical expertise. 'Those are the bones of a goat, not a woman,' he scoffed and was then slightly taken aback when he and his wife were summarily hustled out of the door.

In a similar way he upset the ecclesiastical authorities on a visit to a European cathedral many years later. Like every other visitor he was shown a patch on the floor stained with the blood of a martyr, which appeared, as if by a miracle, fresh every day. Again the Dean of Westminster was sceptical and drawing on his broad and slightly eccentric knowledge of physiology, he dipped a finger in the blood, tasted it and calmly demolished several hundred years of innocent faith with the stark announcement, 'I can tell you what it is; it's bat's urine.'

Though I couldn't claim to be able to recognize the taste of bat's urine, I have eaten the animal itself. There's a restaurant in Ton Buri on the opposite bank to Bangkok in Thailand whose speciality is bat. At the rear of the restaurant there is a large cage in which the creatures hang upside down. You are invited to inspect this cage rather in the manner of choosing trout, crab or lobsters from a fish tank. Having chosen your dinner, its throat is then cut and you are handed a glass of warm blood as an aperitif – not frightfully nice. The bat itself, however is delicious – rather gamey and of a quite delightful texture.

The marvels of modern engineering in New York city held little appeal to Lord Balfour during a visit he made to the Big Apple near the end of his life. The Empire State Building was nearing completion and every VIP was treated to an enthusiastic tour. Balfour was told its height, how many windows there were, how many tons of steel and concrete had been used in its construction and the astonishingly short time it had taken to build. 'And it's practically indestructible by fire,' concluded his guide triumphantly.

'What a pity,' muttered Balfour.

Today the Manhattan skyline has developed a sort of mature majesty all of its own. You need to go west to find the latest eccentricities in American architecture.

I had met Liberace in Australia some years ago and on my next visit to Los Angeles I called at his house in Beverley Hills. It was an astounding house. The carpet started at the main gate and then continued along the drive and up the steps to the front door. From there you looked down on what at first appeared to be an immaculately manicured lawn. Then you realized that that was carpet too. Every day they hoovered the lawn!

There were pianos everywhere and candelabra such as you wouldn't believe – or would you? My favourite of his many pictures was in his mother's room – a large oil painting of the Pope with Liberace kneeling at his feet kissing his ring. But as always with Liberace one was totally won over by his own humour. It was best summed up by a framed sign just inside the door saying, 'Too much of a good thing – is wonderful!'

I suppose the most amazing house I have been to in Los Angeles belonged to an Armenian refuse collector. In LA they put out the refuse collection to private tender and one assumes he must have collected it terribly well because he was hugely rich. He had built a ranch house down the San Fernando valley by blowing the top off a mountain. Here he lived together with some twenty horses. I suppose it was not so much the house that was so incredible but rather the stables. They were without doubt the Hilton of the equine world. Like Liberace, my friend had laid green grass-like carpet between the loose boxes; there was air-conditioning; rows of crystal chandeliers and each horse had its name on its door in gold, but what seemed to be so particularly civilized was that within each stall there was stereophonic sound. Being in California, they were naturally enough played Country and Western music – except for the mares with foals, and they were played lullabies.

Cross the Atlantic, on the other hand, and our American visitors are equally bemused by the sights that they encounter in our 'sceptr'd isle'. Take Stonehenge, for example. There was an American visitor who told her companion, 'The guide says it's been here since time immemorial, but I reckon it's much older than that.' Whereas another traveller from those parts returned to the megalithic ring with a friend and remarked as they were going round, 'It hasn't changed much since we were here five years ago.'

At least she knew what they were looking at. Down in Glastonbury a small group of American ladies, finishing their sandwiches and planning how to pass the time before the coach left, decided to potter round the streets. But one of them thought otherwise, 'I'm gonna stay right here and write my postcards. You go off round the town and tell me about it after . . . Where are we anyway?'

Not that questions like this are the preserve of overseas visitors. In the days before the Prince of Wales married Lady Diana Spencer and the society pages were filled with speculation on whom he might choose as his bride, an English visitor to Blenheim Palace displayed a wonderfully maverick view of British history past and present.

If nothing else, the palace is a hymn to the military exploits of John Churchill, the first Duke of Marlborough. Several of the state rooms are decorated with huge tapestries of his various victories and mementoes from these battles, most notably Blenheim itself, crop up throughout the guided tour. Nevertheless this chap came to the end of his visit and whispered to the guide confidentially, 'Prince Charles is going round with the young lady of the house, I believe?'

The guide politely suggested that he might have been confusing the Duke of Marlborough's eldest daughter with Lady Jane Wellesley, daughter of the Duke of Wellington.

'Yeh, that's right,' said the visitor.

'But this isn't his home,' the guide explained delicately.

'Isn't it?'

'No . . . the Duke of *Marlborough* lives here.'

'Does he? Well, where am I then?'

'Blenheim Palace . . . you know . . . I was telling you about the battle as we went round.'

'Oh . . . yeh,' said the visitor walking off towards the exit. 'The Duke of Marlborough, Battle of Trafalgar . . . 1815.'

A little knowledge is a dangerous thing, particularly when commenting loudly on gardening. Blenheim is also justly famous for its park, about which another visitor enthused to her friend, 'Isn't it lovely? Of course, you know, it was designed by Capability Smith.'

Down the road the dreaming spires of Oxford have had their peace disturbed for years by hordes of tourists trooping round from one crumbling stone façade to another. The porter on duty at Jesus College one sunny afternoon had his peace disturbed by a diffident American who enquired reverently, 'Excuse me . . . er . . . would it be possible to see the . . . the *actual* room?'

Back in the last century another party of Americans was being guided round the university by the eminent scholar and parodist C. S. Calverley. At the time he was going through one of his frequent periods of disagreement with the equally talented scholar, Benjamin Jowett, Master of his old college, Balliol, and when the party arrived outside, Calverley paused in front of the Master's lodgings.

'This, ladies and gentlemen,' he announced, 'is Balliol College, reckoned to be the second oldest college in Oxford. The head of this college is the Master. The present Master is the celebrated Professor Jowett. That is Professor Jowett's study.'

Then, picking up a pebble, he tossed it at the bay window above him, which opened a moment later to reveal Jowett red-faced and furious. 'And that,' concluded Calverley, 'is Professor Jowett.'

Visits of this sort are frequently more rewarding for the guide than the guided. A tourist returning after a morning 'doing the colleges' was asked by his guide whether he would be returning for the afternoon's instalment. 'No, thank you,' he replied. 'I'm stone blind already.'

Some never even get started. I heard of an undergraduate who was stopped as he was crossing Magdalen Bridge by an American driving a rented car who asked, 'Hey, kid, where's the university?'

The young man began to explain that it was lying all around him; that no single building could be defined as the university proper; that one of the charms and attractions of Oxford was that it consisted of a number of independent colleges that collectively formed the whole; that . . .

'OK, OK, forget it,' snapped his questioner. 'Where's the Cotswolds?'

In fairness to so many visitors from the United States they often have far shorter holidays than most of us are allowed, which means that their itineraries are invariably very tight.

There's a story of an American couple in Paris, spending their morning in the Louvre and moving with more determination than appreciation through the galleries. 'What time is it?' asked the wife.

'What's the name of this painting?' said her husband.

'It says "Mona Lisa",' she replied.

'Then it's quarter after eleven,' he told her, 'if we're on time.'

The appearance, even of famous public buildings, can be surprisingly deceptive to foreign eyes. Lady Astor once encountered a young American sailor staring in bewilderment at the façade of the Palace of Westminster and asked him, 'Would you like to go inside?'

'You're the sort of broad my mother told me to avoid,' he said, moving smartly away.

Outside the same imposing edifice a couple of tourists were overheard discussing the Mother of Parliaments. 'What is it?' asked one of them.

'Well, I'm not sure,' said the other. 'But it must be either Oxford or Cambridge.'

There's also the charming account of two more American ladies standing in front of the statue of Achilles in Hyde Park with one saying to her companion, 'No, dear, Big Ben is a clock.'

In 1925 the real Big Ben and the clock tower that houses it were offered for sale to wealthy tourists and went for £1,000. Buckingham Palace fetched twice that price and an oil tycoon from Texas wrote out a cheque for £6,000 and handed it to the 'surveyor from the ministry' in exchange for Nelson's column. Only when the demolition firm whose name he had been given demurred from dismantling one of London's most prominent landmarks did the buyer suspect that he had been duped.

The 'surveyor' who had instigated the 'sale' was a Scottish conman and one-time actor by the name of Arthur Fergusson. He found that the monument-selling business paid considerably better than the stage and, after his success in London, took himself off to New York. There he rented out the White House for the down payment of $100,000 to cover the first year's rent and almost sold the Statue of Liberty to an Australian who thought it would look nice at the entrance to Sydney harbour, though this was the deal that turned sour and cost Fergusson five years in gaol.

Royalty presents the visitor with a fresh batch of perplexities. On a tour of Hatfield House a couple of tourists passed a cabinet and stopped to look at the objects inside. 'It says here that these stockings were worn by Queen Elizabeth,' commented one of them.

'Surely not,' replied the other. 'They must mean her mother.'

At Warwick Castle several years ago a woman pausing in front of a portrait of Henry VIII was overheard saying to her husband, 'Doesn't he look like that actor Keith Michell in the television series?' Which reminds me of the time when, together with Dame Anna Neagle, I was having lunch at Government House in Melbourne, Australia. Behind the governor's chair there was a large picture of the youthful Queen Victoria. Anna suddenly noticed it and said in that charmingly innocent way of hers, 'Oh look, she's wearing the dress that I wore when I played the part.'

Taking the traveller's credibility to the extreme is the case of the woman visiting a bazaar in Cairo where she was shown the actual skull of Cleopatra, on display as a special attraction. Beside it lay a smaller skull. Whose was that, she enquired.

'That's Cleopatra's skull too – when she was a child,' was the inscrutable reply.

Faith is a wonderful thing and blind faith is something else, as was proved when over a hundred Irish holidaymakers flew from Dublin to see the Pope in Rome. Unfortunately they had booked their flight before finding out that the Pope was planning to visit Ireland at the same time. In spite of this most of them still set off on their pilgrimage.

There can be a certain lack of vision as well in sticking too closely to the safe and familiar. After Prince Rainier had been shown round the Houston Astrodome which covers an area of nine acres, he was asked by his Texan hosts, who clearly had little knowledge of the principality, how he would like to have the Astrodome back home in Monaco. 'I should like it very much,' he said diplomatically. 'Then we could be the world's only indoor country.'

For me, and indeed I am sure for anyone who visits it, the Taj Mahal is one of the most romantic sights on earth. Coward may have given Amanda the nagging doubt in *Private Lives* that it might look like a biscuit box, but under the moonlight it's unbeatable – unless you had the misfortune to share that precious moment with the tourist who announced in a rasping Brooklyn accent, 'If this had been in America, it would have been floodlit.'

She would have been in good company with the lady overheard complaining as she struggled up to the Parthenon, 'You'd have thought with all these tourists about they'd have built an elevator', and with the visitor to Caernarvon Castle who asked why they'd built such a splendid place so near the railway station.

The same masterly lack of understanding was displayed by a correspondent to the *Guardian* who joined the debate over the raising of the temple of Abu Simbel when it was threatened with flooding, following the completion of the Aswan High Dam twenty years ago. He wondered whether it was certain that the temples would be better preserved in the open air. Might not submerging them in water be better, he asked, adding, 'Would it not be possible every hundred years or so to let the water out to see how they are getting on?'

Last year my wife and I sailed down from Aswan to Luxor just as all was being made ready for the great production of *Aida* in the temple of Karnak. To our amazement we discovered that here, in a country where the earliest stone buildings were constructed and where the Great Pyramid of Cheops still remains the largest stone building in the world, they had, in 1987, to fly in a team of Korean workmen to repair the stone wall to the river bank.

Possibly the most remarkable approach to historical travel was that of the Abbé Fourmont who set out to obliterate the wonders of the ancient world after he had inspected them! In 1729 he recorded, 'For the last month, thirty and sometimes forty or sixty workers have been smashing, destroying, exterminating the town of Sparta . . . Sparta is the fifth city of Morea that I have pulled down . . . I did not spare Argos or Phylasia.'

Running a close second was an official announcement from the War Office thirty years ago that beauty spots associated with Robin Hood were going to be protected from damage by the creation of a tank training ground in Sherwood Forest.

When in Rome . . .

OVER THE YEARS I have appeared on television in an assortment of ecclesiastical comedy series. In one year in fact I played an Anglican vicar fourteen times and a Catholic monk seven. Once, memorably, on Christmas Day I played a nun as well – a sight it was said that was nearly enough to make Danny La Rue reach for his trousers.

In my experience, however, the hazards of appearing both in Catholic and Protestant series are, one can only say, manifold.

For instance, I once had to fly to Rome to film a sequence for my 'Oh Brother' series in St Peter's Square.

Whilst the cameras were being set up I wandered away in my monastic robes to inspect the great basilica. *En route*, I met a very charming Englishman who stopped me and asked whether I would mind having my photograph taken with his equally charming daughter. There seemed to be no particular problem involved, so I put one arm . . . or perhaps two . . . around her, whilst Pa happily snapped away.

As I started to return to my film unit, I felt an unfriendly hand on my shoulder. When I turned round I discovered that it was attached to the equally unfriendly arm of a Vatican policeman. He indicated that I should accompany him and as his companion was one of those Swiss Guard chaps carrying a very long spike, I decided I had little choice. I was taken across the square and put into a singularly dreary cell somewhere beneath the Curia. It was there that I discovered that I had been 'shopped', I believe the word is, by a nun. Apparently she had decided that by wrapping my arms around a young lady I was not only behaving in a thoroughly unmonkly way but was also most decidedly carrying Christian love too far.

The police demanded to know my identity. I told them

that I was an actor, which didn't impress them terribly, and that I was working with the BBC, which seemed to impress them still less. They then went to look for my film crew, but my gallant producer, seeing my arrest, had fled back to the hotel, taking the unit with him. The BBC, he asserted, couldn't get involved.

Unfortunately, the Chief of Police turned out to be an Anglophobe of the first order. It seemed that whilst serving in the Italian army he had been captured by the British in the Western Desert, and he had then spent the rest of the war working on a potato farm near Wigan. This experience seemed to have soured him against the race in general and me in particular. My trouble was that I had absolutely no way of identifying myself. I was wearing this rather grotty robe (the real monks these days wear lovely silk and mohair outfits), a quick crucifix and some rather ill-chosen rosary beads, whilst on my head rested my BBC-issue pink plastic tonsure, held on by ladies' hair grips. This last mentioned object seemed to offend them most and it was removed from my head and placed on the police station table – to act as Exhibit 'A'.

As time went by I became even more pompous than usual and demanded to see my consul and/or ambassador, all to no avail. My producer refused to answer the telephone and as they seemed to be getting bored with me, they popped me back into my cell.

Some eight hours later a timely miracle happened in the shape of an Irish Dominican monk. He had just returned from leave to County Cork, and presumably had spent the whole time locked to his sister's television set, for he was able to account for me. The Chief of Police then turned decidedly more cheery and my release was arranged. They took away my robes, handed me a blanket – and told me not to make a habit of it.

Having made good my getaway from the Eternal City, I flew back to continue filming in England. Within moments of the cameras beginning to turn, I was hit in the face with an ecclesiastical plank. This whacked me hard around the

face, removed a couple of teeth and blackened one eye. I
was taken to the nearest hospital where the Indian doctor
who examined me only had recently arrived from Delhi. He
asked me to tell him exactly what had happened. I had a go.

'Well, doctor?' I said, as he wrote it all down. 'I was in
this church d'you see, standing on a plank balanced on a log
in front of the altar.'

For some reason he asked me to repeat this. I did.

'And then, doctor, there were these two fat monks standing
on top of the altar.'

'Did you say *monks*?' he asked.

'Well, actually, I did, and these two monks jumped off the
top of the altar on to the end of the plank in the hope of
sending me up . . .'

'Sending you up?'

'Yes, that is exactly right, sending me up into the air, so
that I could grab hold of the chandelier.'

'What chandelier was that?'

'The one in the church that I intended swinging on, but it
didn't work out that way. When the monks jumped, the
plank slewed round and bashed me, as you can see.'

At this point, curiously enough, the good doctor decided
to stop writing.

I never did discover the identity of that nun but I like to
think it may have been the selfsame one who was the first to
be assigned to security work at St Peter's. She had been given
the job of vetting the clothing of visitors and making sure
that no immodestly dressed tourists passed the sacred portal,
because it was felt that a nun was less likely to give in to a
pretty girl's arguments than a man. However, after only a
few weeks on the job she had to be relieved of her post after
suffering a nervous breakdown as a result of refusing entry
to thousands of women clad in miniskirts, see-through
blouses and other revealing attire, not to mention constant
jostling from photographers trying to get a lensful and less
than charitable remarks from the press.

A good century and a half before I fell foul of the Vatican
authorities another English visitor, Charles Waterton of

Walton Hall, Yorkshire, had a spot of bother with Pope
Pius VII when he and a friend scaled the imposing façade of
St Peter's and put their gloves on top of the lightning conductor. The Pope was absolutely livid and immediately ordered
that they should be removed. However, none of his staff felt
inclined to risk the ascent and in the end it fell to one man
to soothe the papal wrath and undertake the dangerous
climb. That was none other than Charles Waterton.

Attitudes to authority abroad can be wildly divergent. On
the one hand are those who only have to catch sight of a
foreign policeman (or in the case of some ladies, be sighted
by them) before finding themselves under arrest. Set against
them are travellers like the correspondent to the *News Chron-
icle* who wrote, 'I can't understand how it is that English-
women keep on getting themselves locked up in Spain. When
I was there, I thought the policemen were wonderful, so
helpful, so courteous. And they wore such elegant hats. I
never had cause to argue with, or to hit, one of them.'

It's not just in sartorial convention that nations differ;
some of the laws the traveller encounters can land him or
her in hot water, especially if they are as bizarre as a few
that I have come across. Out in the Middle East it's forbidden
to eat snakes in Iraq on Sundays or to play drums in Oman.
Hunting camels is illegal in the State of Arizona, while riding
one through the streets of Vancouver is liable to have you
run in by the Mounties. Not long ago there was still a
ban on pushing bathchairs three abreast in at least two of
London's royal parks. Apparently it's illegal to drink water
in the beer parlours of Saskatchewan, to hang male and
female underwear on the same washing-line in Minnesota or
to sell antifreeze to Indians in the province of Quebec.
Edward Gibbon may have reminded us that 'The laws of a
nation form the most instructive portion of its history' but
they also show that somewhere along the line somebody had
some pretty old notions about what was right and wrong. I
mean it wasn't that long ago that it was felt necessary to write
into the Nigerian constitution a clause stating that *coups
d'état* were illegal!

When it comes to writing international laws the problems are compounded. Ken Tynan must have spoken for many of his countrymen when he contemplated our entry into the Common Market and remarked less than enthusiastically, 'I do not see the EEC as a great love affair. It is more like nine middle-aged couples with failing marriages meeting at a Brussels hotel for a group grope.'

This view was echoed by a speaker at an agricultural dinner held in Sussex, who informed his audience that while there are fifty-six words in the Lord's Prayer, 297 words in the Ten Commandments, and 300 words in the American Declaration of Independence, an EEC directive on the export of duck eggs runs to a modest 26,911!

Little wonder that there are those who regard the prospect of 'open' frontiers within the community after 1992 with a wry smile.

To add insult to injury, as some would have it, we're all going to be issued with European passports. One wonders how these might circumvent just a few of the problems that have arisen with the good old model issued by Her Britannic Majesty's Secretary of State for Foreign and Commonwealth Affairs that has been such a comfort to so many of Her subjects in far-flung corners of the globe. To put off the evil day when I shall have to sport the standard European passport I have just acquired a new bumper eighty-page, dark navy blue, greater crested British passport valid for ten years. That should see me out.

Less than twenty years ago there were demands in Parliament for spelling tests in English and French (the language of diplomacy and passports) to be given to staff in the passport office after a number of orthographic errors had come to light. One issue of passports bore a non-existent French word. A batch of Visitor's Passports mis-spelt Gibraltar and the MP who raised the matter directly with the Passport Office received the reply, 'Have we, really? We spelt Sweden wrong in the last issue.'

Little problems like this are nothing new. As long ago as 1915 an applicant for a British passport filled in the form provided for the purpose and, asked to describe his face, entered the word 'intelligent'. You'll appreciate then his annoyance when he received his new passport and found that some nameless official at Petty France had substituted for his own facial description the altogether more prosaic characterization 'oval'.

I suppose the only compensation is that the bureaucracy of travel is universal. I like the aplomb of the lady hiker holidaying somewhere in central Europe who reached the top of a mountain track and found a frontier post she hadn't been expecting. The guard on duty asked to see her papers. Her passport was back in her hotel and her only possession that looked vaguely official was her Post Office savings book, so she proffered this. The guard looked at it sternly, flicked through the pages and commented that she always seemed to be going to 'Ondemand' and hoped that his country would be a nice change. Then he handed back the 'passport' and wished her a pleasant stay.

(In the same vein is the experience of another lady who asked the way to the Urdu section of the BBC World Service and was sent by the commissionaire to a nearby hairdresser where she could get an 'airdo.)

Passing through customs can cause a special type of problem, particularly if you're bending the rules ever so slightly. There was a chap I heard of bringing through a very expensive watch and a pair of magnificent earrings for his wife who was stopped in the Green channel and asked by a rather aggressive customs officer whether he really had nothing to declare.

'Nothing at all, sir?' asked the excise man, eyeing him suspiciously. 'No extra spirits or tobacco? No pornographic literature?'

'Certainly not,' stammered the traveller with relief. 'I don't even own a pornograph.'

A barrister friend of mine, one Gilbert Rodway, was spotted by the customs officers going through Heathrow the other day and was called to one side. 'Excuse me, sir, have you got anything to declare?' asked the customs officer.

'No,' said my chum.

'Well, I would like to point out that you are wearing two watches.'

'No, I'm not,' said Gilbert.

'I'm sorry, sir, but I can see them.'

'You're quite wrong,' said my friend. 'I am wearing four.' Whereupon he rolled up his sleeve and revealed three solid gold Piaget wristwatches and a diamond-encrusted Cartier. He didn't of course have to declare them, being resident in Hong Kong.

Then there was the Arab gentleman spotted at Heathrow, resplendent in traditional flowing garments and surrounded by his huge family, who was busily cutting Marks & Spencer labels off a large pile of clothing bursting from several suitcases.

Blessed with less presence of mind was the group of illegal immigrants hidden inside a lorry that arrived at Dover and drew up at the customs hall for its statutory inspection. The customs officer looking it over suspected that there might be something fishy going on and, knocking on the side, called out, 'Are you all right in there?'

'Yes, thank you,' chanted the twenty men secreted inside.

Having had the good fortune to have been entertained by a number of extremely wealthy men during my travels in the Far East I heard with amusement the story of the first visit to Britain paid by a member of a powerful Chinese trading family whose command of English unfortunately did not match the scale of his fortune. At the immigration desk at Heathrow he was asked repeatedly, 'How much money have you got?' which he greeted with blank incomprehension.

Finally, through the agency of crude sign language, the penny dropped and the Chinese visitor leant across to the immigration officer and whispered, 'How much you want?'

For almost half a century travelling expenses dogged a former private in the US army, one Edward H. Denny. Having been discharged in the Philippines in 1899, after serving in the Spanish American War, he had a rather tricky time getting home and submitted a claim for the equivalent of £93 to cover his travel and subsistence expenses. It wasn't until the Second World War had been over a couple of years that he finally received confirmation that his claim had been approved.

The mills of diplomacy, like those of God, grind slowly and exceeding small. When a case of identifying a certain Monsieur Dussart came to the notice of the Belgian consul in Miami some years ago, he had this ready solution, 'If he can present himself to me and establish he is who he is, I can sign and verify he is he. Then we can send the certificate to Brussels and find out very quickly whether he is dead or alive.'

The same blinding logic greeted an anxious passenger on the London underground who found himself locked in Cannon Street tube station one night after he had got off the last train and stopped to make a phone call. The lights were switched off and, trying all the exit gates, he found them locked. So groping his way through the dark, he found the telephone he had been using and dialled 999. The operator answered, listened to his predicament and then told him, 'This number's for life and death cases. You must dial "0",' and put down the receiver.

The man locked in the station did what he was told, dialled '0' and spoke to the same operator, who duly informed the City police!

Travel above ground isn't necessarily any more straight-forward. A London Transport passenger who wanted to go to Hampstead Heath got on to a number 24 bus at Tottenham Court Road in spite of the fact that its destination sign read 'Oxford Circus'. He asked the conductor where it was actually heading. 'Hampstead Heath,' he replied.

'But the sign on the front says Oxford Circus,' pointed out the passenger.

'It says India on the tyres, but we're not going to Calcutta,' was the conductor's laconic reply.

In 1976 bus passengers in Staffordshire ran into an even more bewildering example of travel bureaucracy when people wishing to travel between Hanley and Bagnall noticed that buses were regularly passing would-be passengers queue-ing at bus-stops all along the route. Complaints were made to the bus authorities, who responded via one of their spokes-men with the astonishing comment that if buses stopped to pick up passengers, they couldn't keep up with the timetable.

Service like this stems from a fine tradition in public transport worldwide. One pocket guide to our capital city offered visitors the nugget of advice, 'If you are lost in London, telephone 222 1234 (London Transport), tell them where you are and they will tell you where to go.'

On the concourse of the main railway station in Amster-dam the Dutch Railways travel bureau carried a sign which was literally the last word in tourist information. Printed in Dutch and English, it read, 'No train information. No boat information. No international tickets. No maps of the city. Tourist and Hotel Information – not here.'

Just about as helpful is the sort of advice to tourists which would have made Gerard Hoffnung envious. Gems like that offered in one issue of the Pan-Am in-flight magazine which told readers that 'with few exceptions tickets are always available at London theatre box offices on the day of the performance or soon thereafter.'

Ten years ago there was an almighty downpour in Jeddah in Saudi Arabia which came as quite a surprise to both visitors and residents in a country famed for its deserts and without a single river within its frontiers. But better was to come when the evening news bulletin informed listeners, 'We regret we are unable to give you the weather. We rely on weather reports from the airport, which is closed because of the weather. Whether we are able to give the weather tomorrow depends on the weather.'

At the other temperature extreme comes the story of a course in Arctic survival for would-be explorers in the polar regions which was due to be held in upper New York State, but had to be cancelled due to inclement weather.

For anyone who's ever missed a train, jumped on to a wrong bus or forgotten minor details like time changes be-tween different countries, it's comforting to know that seasoned travellers can also run into little problems now and then.

Even the celebrated scientists who travelled down under with Captain Cook weren't without fault. Among the extraordinary species of animals they discovered in Australia was one that jumped along on its back legs, using its tail, in a series of giant hops. Never having ever seen anything like it in their lives they asked a passing aborigine what the peculiar animal was. 'Kangaroo,' he replied, and kangaroo it has been called in English ever since.

What they overlooked was that in the aborigine's language 'kangaroo' actually meant 'I don't know.'

Most travel wouldn't be travel without the use of maps and any road map of this country will demonstrate the extraordinary passion the Romans had for building roads all over their conquered lands – long, straight roads with typically Italian names like Watling Street. A couple of hundred years ago a considerable flurry of excitement erupted in mapping circles with the discovery of an early 'guidebook' to this country with the catchy little title *De Situ Britanniae* which included a very early map along with a written description of the British Isles. The author was a previously unknown minor cleric of the fourteenth century, one Richard of Cirencester.

His book had come to light through the labours (quite literally as it turned out) of a 24-year-old teacher of English in Denmark called Charles Julius Bertram. He showed his 'find' to the scholar and first secretary of the London Society, William Stukeley, who rather too enthusiastically rushed it into print.

Eager to catch some of the limelight, other scholars jumped on the bandwagon, enthusing on the new light shed on early British history: Richard of Cirencester's book mentioned more than a hundred roads, settlements and individuals referred to nowhere else.

A Manchester historian, John Whitaker, used it as his principal source when he wrote his *Antiquarian Romance* and even Edward Gibbon felt moved to quote it in his *Decline and Fall of the Roman Empire* and commented, 'Although it may not seem probable that he wrote it from the manuscript of a Roman general, he shows a genuine knowledge of antiquity very extraordinary for a monk of the fourteenth century.'

As it turned out, Gibbon was a good deal closer to the truth than he might have cared to know, though his blushes and those of other eminent scholars were spared: it took over a century for the truth about Richard of Cirencester to come to light. It was the German scholar Karl Wex who noticed certain inconsistencies in Richard's manuscript, most notable of which was that his quotations from Tacitus came from an edition of the Roman historian's work printed two hundred years after Richard had died! Further investigations revealed that the whole manuscript had actually been cobbled together from chunks written by a number of Roman historians, augmented by some of the 'author's' own colourful flights of fancy.

However, by the time it was revealed that a considerable number of leading scholars had been taken for a ride, the damage had been done. The Ordnance Survey had dutifully printed all of the 'new information' on their maps and as recently as the beginning of this century other works were still being published with bogus 'revelations' from *De Situ Britanniae.*

Sometimes errors occur quite innocently. During a map-making survey of the coast of Alaska in 1849 one of the British cartographers noticed that none of the information available to him gave the name of a prominent peninsula he was charting. All he could do was write 'Name?' alongside it, so that the correct name could be ascertained back at his London headquarters. However, the draftsman working from his survey misread this and thinking that the cartographer had written Nome, gave this as the name of the promontory. As a result, this and the nearby city that grew up in the gold rush at the end of the century have been called Nome ever since.

(On reflection, British travellers have often displayed a

rather curious attitude to the possibilities offered by the New World. Not long after the first colonists crossed the Atlantic from these shores, the Earl of Stirling was able to rent the whole of Canada from the Crown for a penny a year.)

Less than fifty years before the discovery of 'Nome' the far north-west of the USA beckoned the indefatigable explorer Thomas Nuttall, who ranks in the annals of early American exploration as one of the less august frontiersmen.

Nuttall was a botanist by training and, if experience is anything to go by, one more at home in the laboratory than the backwoods. In 1812 he led an expedition into the wilds in the course of which he managed to get himself lost at regular intervals. His colleagues took to lighting beacons to lead him back to camp at night. When he failed to appear altogether one evening they organized a search party and set off to find him. Nuttall saw them approaching, mistook them for a band of Indians and ran off. His chums spent three days trying to bring him back before he found his way back to camp more by accident than design. In fact Nuttall had more to fear from himself than from Indians. He became so exhausted on another occasion when he had lost his way that he lay down for a rest and was discovered in this parlous state by an Indian out hunting. Far from inflicting harm on Nuttall, the explorer cut such a pitiful figure that the Indian picked him up and delivered him by canoe back to his long-suffering colleagues.

Across the continent in Upper New York state stand the forty-six peaks that make up the Adirondack range. Climbing all of these was the goal that Keith Solomon from across the forty-ninth parallel in Ontario set himself – and he jolly nearly succeeded too. At the age of fifty-eight, forty-five of them were under his belt and he was less than five hundred feet from the summit of the forty-sixth, Mount Saddleback, when fate and physiology combined to rob him of success and he was felled by a heart attack.

Somewhat more fortunate, though at the time it might not have seemed that way, was the fate of a mountaineer on Mont Blanc in 1861. He was one of an experienced party of climbers on their way up to the top of Europe's highest mountain. After breakfast one morning he took himself off discreetly for a few minutes to spend a penny. It was probably rather chilly up there fiddling with buttons and braces, in any event he can't have fully adjusted his dress, because he slipped, fell and started sliding down a precipice. In the words of the *Medical Times and Gazette*, 'He slid down 1,500 feet at an angle of 45 deg. by measurement, at a velocity of not less than sixty miles an hour, over frozen snow covered by little peas of ice like hail, and was brought up at a crevasse by the collected snow in his clothes; this was owing to the arrangement of his dress at the time of the accident, his trousers, down, had no doubt saved him by tying his legs together,' – literally caught, as it were, with his pants down.

His descent recalls the unhappy experience of a woman on a skiing holiday in the same area a century later. The mountains offer unparalleled freedom in the pristine expanses of snow and ice but they're not exactly littered with loos. Like so many skiers before her, she had to take emergency measures and with one-piece skiing clothing being what it is, this was quite a performance. The process wasn't made any easier by the fact that she decided to keep her skis on as she squatted behind a rock. This proved to be her undoing.

Slowly, imperceptibly at first, she began sliding. Only when it was too late did she realize what was happening as she emerged from behind her rock, quickly gathering speed. In an agony of indecision, not to say embarrassment, she was soon whizzing down the piste, her centre of gravity low, her skis locked into a perfect parallel by the outfit gathered round her ankles. Fellow skiers swerved in amazement as she swept past, her bottom barely a couple of inches from the hard-packed snow – very barely.

I'm reliably informed that rolling naked in snow does wonders for the system after a sauna, but I can only speculate on this good lady's feelings when a large snowdrift in a wood at the bottom of the ski-run brought her to an unceremonious and decidely refreshing halt.

Among the most famous mountaineering images is the first

photograph taken on the summit of Everest in 1953. It shows
Tenzing, of course; Hillary was the photographer. However,
no companion picture of Hillary was ever taken up there and
in answer to repeated questions as to why this was the case,
Hillary explained that he hadn't asked Tenzing to photograph
him for the delightfully simple reason that, 'as far as I knew,
he had never taken a photograph before, and the summit of
Everest was hardly the place to show him how.'

What a shame. The prospect of the two of them lumbering
about with ice axes and oxygen cylinders on that pinnacle of
rock and ice at the top of the world discussing exposures and
focal lengths, not to mention the inevitable 'Back a bit . . .
back a bit' raises a smile.

I suppose it must be that cool reasoning even in the
moments of greatest personal triumph that sets the seasoned
traveller apart from the eager and wildly over-excited tourist.

On a more mundane but no less relevant level are the day-
to-day considerations of what to wear when travelling. I now
travel in the most comfortable old things imaginable. This
was a lesson that was taught to me some years ago when
I flew with Moira Lister to do a little play with her in
Johannesburg. We had been told that there would be press
and film cameramen waiting for us upon arrival and so I
travelled sartorially immaculate in what I believe is called in
America 'a prestige suit'. (Funny idea that. It's the sort of
suit which is cut so beautifully that one's tailor forbids one
to put anything in its pockets. He says it will 'spoil the line'.
So I end up with a prestige suit and have to carry my glasses
and wallet in a brown paper bag). To my surprise, however,
the glamorous Miss Lister arrived wearing, uncharacteristi-
cally, an old jumper and jeans. Twelve hours later I discovered why. Just before we landed, Moira disappeared into
the loo with a large bag to emerge minutes later in a beautiful
white silk dress; with her long gloves and surmounted by the
most divine picture hat imaginable she looked for all the
world as though she was on her way to Royal Ascot.

The plane touched down. Moira walked down the steps
with the cameras turning and the flashbulbs flashing, looking

a million Rand. Whilst I followed crumpled, faded and decidedly brown round the edges.

Knowing what to pack is also terribly important, though the world has sadly moved on from the era of the handy little book entitled *Notes on an Outfit for India and Hints for the New Arrival* which no doubt supplied much invaluable information to travellers to the sub-continent at the turn of the century. Under the heading *List of Outfit (to be procured in England)* it kicks off with:

Baggage: 2 or more packing cases, hinged and padlocked. 3 steel trunks of different sizes. 2 leather Gladstone bags. 1 canvas trunk. 1 hold-all. 2 hat-boxes.

Greatcoats: 1 thick greatcoat or ulster. 1 thin overcoat or dustcoat.

Waterproofs: 1 regulation military waterproof.

The list continued with other crucial items like: 1 dress suit, thin; 3 plain clothes suits; 6 white Marcella waistcoats; 2 Norfolk jackets; 2 pairs of riding breeches; 1 or more pairs of knickerbockers; 3 dozen shirts; 3 dozen collars; 1½ dozen vests; 12 pairs of assorted footwear; 6 hats; 2 hair-stuffed pillows; 1 pair of binoculars; 1 chart of the voyage; 1 whisky flask; a complete set of cutlery for six; saddlery; musical instruments; pistol; hunting knife; cricket, lawn tennis and racquet bats; and paintbox.

The author thought it was probably better to wait until your arrival before acquiring guns, rifles, despatch boxes, fishing rods, polo sticks and hunting spears.

What amuses me is that barely a paragraph above this impressive catalogue the author had felt fit to caution his readers, 'Natives of India think along different grooves of thought from ours. It does not follow that we are always right. It is true, however, that we are always *practical* [my italics]; hence the need for us in the country.'

Like many Victorian men of science, Sir Francis Galton was another of those travellers who was tireless and unselfish when it came to passing on the benefit of their experience to others. In 1855 he published the *Art of Travel* which was packed with useful tips from breaking a raw egg into a boot before putting it on, to soften the leather, to tracking a bee to its hive by tying a feather to its leg and following the feather. Out in the bush he lists opera glasses and an ear trumpet as invaluable additions to the standard camp kit. Galton also had a high regard for fireworks. 'Of all European inventions,' he commented, 'nothing so impresses and terrifies savages as fireworks, especially rockets. I cannot account for the remarkable effect they produce, but in every land it appears to be the same. A rocket, judiciously sent up, is very likely to frighten off an intended attack and save bloodshed. If a traveller is supplied with any of these, he should never make playthings of them, but keep them for great emergencies.'

But before we're tempted into a supercilious snigger at these earnest excesses, it's worth remembering that Galton once managed to save face in a meeting with an exotically attired and decorated tribal chief near the Zambezi by arriving clad in full hunting pink and riding an ox.

Local Colour

THERE'S AN INCURABLE yearning in most travellers to delve beneath the superficial veneer of tourism and package holidays; to discover the heartbeat of a new country and experience life in the raw there at first hand. Indeed it was such an endeavour that lured me to a country race meeting in Australia several years ago.

I call it a 'country race meeting', but that gives a rather false impression. It was in reality just a stretch of flat ground in a valley surrounded by time-eroded hills.

The only permanent building on the course was the gaol, and by lunchtime there were seven people in it. I said to the policeman who ran the joint, 'How many does it hold?'

'Like twelve.'

'Good Lord,' I replied. 'What happens when it's full?'

'It gets crowded,' he said – and it did!

There were only twenty horses and thirteen races and they went round four at a time in different permutations. It is the only time that I have seen the 4.15 run at 3.30 to allow more time for drinking.

At night I went to what they called a 'Hootenanny', which I suppose roughly might be called a dance – very roughly. It was for those who could still stand up, so it wasn't exactly overpopulated.

Suddenly an enormous man wearing leather trousers, a leather waistcoat and biceps came up to me.

'Would you like to dance with me?' he asked.

I thanked him kindly, but intimated that I was sitting that one out, at which he lurched nearer and standing uncomfortably close shouted, '*I said would you like to dance with me?*'

I again told him that it was indeed frightfully kind, but owing to the lateness of the hour I felt I must decline.

He then drew himself up to his full six feet four, dropping

several tubes in the course of this manoeuvre, and bellowed, 'WHAT'S THE MATTER, DO YOU THINK I AM A POOFTAH?'

I assured him that nothing was further from my thoughts, whereupon he seemed to lose his enthusiasm, for he just slid to the ground, still clutching his Fosters, and went fast asleep!

My first experience of a race meeting in Australia had been somewhat less exciting. It was in 1971 when I first flew into Melbourne. There was a letter waiting for me on arrival inviting me to address four hundred ladies on a race course in a little town some hundred miles away called Bendigo.

For four hundred ladies I would go almost anywhere. Even, indeed, to Bendigo, and as the invitation brought with it the prospect of a country race meeting, I accepted with alacrity. Now my understudy, one Robin Bowering, is equally enthusiastic about the sport of kings, so I asked if he could accompany me. He is a jolly good chap to have around at the races and also if Dame Fortune's smile should turn a little frosty he is generally good for the loan of a fiver as well.

The invitation duly arrived, and a very tasteful example of the printer's art is proved to be:

You are invited to
A GLAMOUR GALA
CHAMPAGNE AND TOM TURKEY LUNCHEON
To Be Held On
THE EPSOM RACE COURSE BENDIGO
in aid of the
Nadegong Home for the Aged Blind

They had kindly said that they would send an aeroplane for me, but come the day of the races, and Melbourne being Melbourne, it was pouring with rain. As the plane couldn't take off, they had to send a car instead. When the car arrived I was waiting with Bowering, clad in our tweeds and carrying binoculars and shooting sticks. We duly climbed aboard and sped off, Bendigo-bound. About a couple of miles along the

The wonderful Wild West—
Joe Bugner was in Las Vegas,
training for the Big Fight. I went
off to get a taste of what things
used to be like

Knock-out to Nimmo! Joe Bugner taking a splash—in Las Vegas

High-rolling in Las Vegas

Chips with everything—in Las Vegas

Words of local wisdom after an all-night gambling session—in Las Vegas

Oh Brother! or a funny thing happened to me in the Vatican

(*Radio Times*)

Tulamarine Freeway the driver turned to me, pointing at my field glasses and shooting stick, and said, 'What have you got those for?' I tried to explain that in England we put our bottoms on these little sticks and then, resting comfortably, point the glasses at the horses so we can enjoy the races.

'Oh, there are no races,' he said.

'What do you mean "no races"?' said I.

'No, mate, it's just that these four hundred shielas meet on the racecourse once a year and have lunch.'

Bowering then lapsed into a heavy sulk all the way along the long road to Bendigo!

When we arrived it was still pouring with rain and the ladies had been forced to adjourn from the racecourse (which was by now under water) and had sought sanctuary in a handily adjacent cattle shed. The shed had the day before housed the local agricultural show and it was, not to put too fine a point on it, decidedly niffy. But Australians are the most remarkably resilient people and I shall long treasure the sight of those four hundred gallant but damp ladies, wearing splendid floral hats and long gloves, sitting on benches in a cattle shed, drinking champagne. Nor will I forget either being introduced to the gathering by the Madam Chairman beneath a sign which still bore the legend 'COWS AND SWINE'.

Since then I seem to have spent an amazing amount of time addressing vast quantities of lunching ladies. My favourite lunch of all was held in the garden of a very gracious home belonging to Lady Curtis in Melbourne. It was in aid of the Royal Overseas League. Now the Royal Overseas League is a splendid bunch of loyalist ladies much given to wearing red, white and blue favours and being suitably patriotic. Before my speech I was taken round the garden by the Madam Vice-President and introduced to the assembled guests.

'Mr Neemo [they always seem to call me Neemo in Australia] would you like to meet . . .'

'Hello,' I said. 'How frightfully nice . . .'

'Mr Neemo, would you like . . .'

'How nice . . .'

'Mr Neemo, would you like . . .'

She didn't get any further for she walked into the swimming pool. Her hat floated on the top like a marker buoy and her elderly hand came up like Excalibur from the waves. But nobody moved. They were all so ashamed that the Madam Vice-President had walked into the swimming pool. So I had to rescue her and wrap her in a blanket and send her home in a taxi.

The Madam Vice-Vice-President then stepped into the breach and continued with the introductions. She was a Miss Macdonald and was covered from head to foot in Macdonald tartan including a tartan bowler hat. The funny thing, though, was that neither Miss Macdonald, nor indeed anyone else, mentioned what had happened. It was as though only I had seen it. I had every sympathy with St Bernadette!

Eventually (and I have told you how resilient Australians are), the Madam Vice-President returned, wearing an even larger hat and slightly longer gloves.

Well, when the time came for me to make my speech I thought I'd better refer in some way to what had occurred, if only to clear the air – or perhaps water.

'Ladies,' I said rather diffidently, 'perhaps after this afternoon the Royal Overseas League ought to be called the Royal Underwater League.'

Not a smile greeted this.

I tried again.

'You know, until today I had always thought walking on the water was a male preserve.'

Again there wasn't even the faintest flicker. I moved on to other things.

Knowing how to adapt to what might be termed 'local conditions' is one of the prerequisites of the experienced traveller.

Some people don't even try, of course. A few years after the last war a smartly dressed Englishwoman was seen stepping off a train at Milan and without a word she proceeded to slap the guard, her porter and the stationmaster. Apprehended by the police she told them haughtily that this was her way of protesting against 'the cold reception given by everybody here'.

In contrast was the reception given to a former British ambassador in Buenos Aires before the war who readily admitted that he had gone to Argentina with one or two prejudices, but had had these dispelled during his first year. As an indication of the esteem with which he held the Argentinians he went as far as saying that he found them 'the most natural, and if I may say so, the most English people I have ever met'.

Before the recent wave of reforms really got underway I found when travelling in China that foreigners like myself were frequently the subject of intense curiosity. It wasn't uncommon, away from the principal tourist sites, to find sizeable crowds gathering to stare at us foreign devils. In one large regional centre the city authorities decided to take decisive steps to curb this wholesale inquisitiveness. It wasn't good for tourism, for one thing. And it showed up the People's Republic for another. Staring at foreigners, it was decreed, undermined China's status as a world force to counter the 'two superpowers' by reflecting her ignorance of the world outside the Middle Kingdom.

Then it was pointed out that staring enviously at foreigners was a sure sign of bourgeois revisionism, which was always a good line in official condemnation.

Finally they put forward the security angle. Such huge crowds gathered round visitors from abroad, it was claimed, that they hampered the work of the police to such an extent that 'class enemies' were free to commit acts of theft.

Decrees were issued, but the staring persisted. That's until the barriers were removed and foreign devils started flocking in with all their lovely bourgeois trappings.

Not that travellers to these shores fail to attract attention at times. Thirty years ago when public morality was, well, a little more moral, a ticket collector in charge of deck chairs round the Serpentine was forced to acknowledge, 'Of course people do their courting in Hyde Park,' with the important qualification, 'Usually it is the foreigners who go a bit far. English couples – well, they know when to stop.'

However, a different sense of decorum prevailed in Green Park, where a chair attendant answered the same enquiry stiffly, 'People always behave themselves here.'

A year or two earlier the splendidly named *Empire News* printed a letter from an outraged reader that highlighted another interesting social divide. 'Our holiday in Blackpool last week was ruined by canoodling couples,' stated the correspondent. 'My husband and I were terribly embarrassed, because we had our two daughters, 14 and 16, with us. For our next holiday (in July) we are going to Bournemouth. You don't see this shameless behaviour in the South.'

Behaviour of an altogether different sort brought an itinerant French martyr into conflict with the police in Jerusalem when he tried to crucify himself on a hill outside the city. Having had himself crucified in seventeen different countries he was understandably a little put out by their veto, exclaiming forcefully, 'I think it's a disgrace that it should be stopped in the place of its origin.'

The police remained unmoved. 'There's no place for stunts like that around here nowadays,' commented a spokesman.

From the time of the British mandate in Palestine comes a rather different perception of the Holy Land and some of its key sites, at least according to a travel article that appeared in *Sphere* with the interesting observation, 'The Church of the Annunciation, lying in the southern quarter, is built on the foundations of a crusader's shrine, and is one of the sights of Nazareth, the town that has suddenly leapt into the news with the murder of the British officials.'

In spite of our imperial legacy, it can't be claimed that the British have an all-embracing knowledge of the world's cultures, even at a popular level. A few years ago a series of amusing vodka advertisements appeared offering drinkers a special insight into hidden truths if they tossed back a measure or two. One that had an all too brief life on the hoardings ran along the lines of, 'I thought the Kama Sutra was an Indian restaurant until I discovered Smirnoff.'

However, a market survey that followed this revealed that sixty per cent of those interviewed thought that the Kama Sutra actually was an Indian restaurant and the advertisement was discontinued.

Appearances can be deceptive, especially when it comes to restaurants. The formal notice announcing the licence transfer of one in north London carried further revealing information. Mr Wu's Chinese Restaurant, formerly owned by Wu Wai Wang, was acquired by Kyriacos Panayouto and Demetrious Antoniou under the new name of the Highland Angus Eating House.

No wonder visitors claim to have trouble understanding the British diet. Just to confuse things further, down on the south coast a health food shop was advertising the cosmopolitan-sounding 'Zimbabwe live Bulgarian apricot natural goat's milk yoghurt'.

The provision of delicacies like this might go some way to explaining the diffidence felt by some visitors when ordering food here. An American tourist, ordering breakfast at a respected country hotel in the Cotswolds was asked how he would like his boiled egg and replied hesitatingly, 'Medium rare.'

At least we aren't alone in baffling our visitors. Around the world you come across a wonderful selection of 'whiskies' that have about as much to do with Scotch as the brand of sticky tape so popular in America – many of them taste as about as appealing as well. Apparently there was a Japanese whisky on sale in Kenya bearing the impressive name 'House of Lords' which assured the drinker it was 'as drunk in the House of Lords since 1066'.

In *Private Lives* Noël Coward has the memorable lines on the delights of dining abroad, of eating strange foods and making strange noises afterwards, based no doubt on experiences from his own extensive travels. While he was staying at Raffles Hotel in Singapore he discovered a couple of remarkable American guests whose conversation so enthralled him that he endeavoured to sit at the adjoining table at every meal. Among the many nuggets he gleaned was the comment at lunch one day, 'I found out what that white stuff was we had in Japan. It was rice.'

I'm one of those fortunate people who – like the good Dr Buckland (he of the iron constituion and pioneering gastronomic predilection) – can eat almost anything that comes my way. I'm never really ill. Ever since I started travelling, I've subjected my stomach to the most unlikely things. In Australia I've happily dug witchetty grubs out of logs of wood and eaten them live.

When I'm in Oman we always swim out from the shore towing behind us a bottle of Moët et Chandon to accompany the live oysters that we prise off the rocks.

One of my favourite dishes, which I always have when I'm in Hong Kong, is ducks' tongues. You get these on a plate and eat them with chopsticks. But when you put them in, two or three at a time, they're quite noticeably little intruders within your mouth and they're also quite noticeably tongues. So eating them is rather like a French kiss in triplicate.

One of the menus that most fired my imagination was that of the Chokchai restaurant, in Thailand, the one where I first tasted bat. This has a whole section devoted to wild animals. You can have 'Fried Crocodile tail', 'Roasted Langur', 'Boar in hot chilli', 'Mountain Lizard' (that's very nice). The 'Cobra Meat' is very tasty too. There's a 'Tiger Meat Salad', should you fancy something nice and cold. On the menu when I was once there they were offering Elephants' Feet, but you had to order those twenty-four hours in advance, so that they could defrost them.

Over the page was a section with the curious heading 'Misalliance Plates'. There, apart from the obvious things like 'Fried Misalliance Pork', were the rather mysteriously named 'Fried Eight Fairy' and also 'Steamed Three Fairy in earthenpot'. Under the same heading you could also treat yourself to 'Rolled egg with pork and sugar pen' or the equally appetising 'Fried convolvulvuvuls [sic]'.

Under 'Frog' you might excite a jaded palate with 'Salt and sour frog soup' or 'Fried frog with holy basil leaves'. Basil features quite a lot on the menu, though seldom more strikingly than in 'Fried dried fish with holy boly holy basil leaves'.

Among the poultry dishes 'Chicken leg in reg gravy' caught my eye, as did 'Steamed sweet and sour serpent-nerd fish' listed under 'River Fish'.

I've just come back from Korea and there a great delicacy is 'kinchi', which is essentially cabbage. There are many different ways of cooking and preparing this with all kinds of herbs. In fact they've even got a museum dedicated to cabbage where you can go and see the many different ways in which cabbage has been used through the centuries. In Korea a man's wealth is easily discerned by the number of jars of kinchi he has outside his house. Even in trade union negotiations you negotiate how many jars should be given to the workers over and above their salary.

Relatively familiar foreign foods can cause a certain amount of confusion on this side of the Channel and thirty years ago, when far fewer of us strayed across the water to sample the delights of Continental fare, it was still possible for the BBC to bring off its celebrated feature on the Swiss Spaghetti Harvest which was broadcast during *Panorama* on April Fool's Day 1957.

Against a background of gentle violin music and a peaceful Alpine landscape Richard Dimbleby cheerfully explained the circumstances leading to the recent bumper spaghetti crop which held the promise of being one of the best in recent years, now that the dangers of a late March frost had been safely passed.

'Spaghetti cultivation here in Switzerland,' he continued, 'is not of course carried out on anything like the scale of the Italian industry. Many of you, I'm sure, will have seen pictures of the vast spaghetti plantations in the Po Valley. For the Swiss, however, it tends to be a family affair. Another reason why this may be a bumper year lies in the virtual diappearance of the spaghetti weevil, the tiny creature whose depredations have caused much concern in the past.'

Turning to the actual process of curing the crop, he explained, 'Many people are often puzzled by the fact that spaghetti is produced at such uniform lengths. But this is the result of many years of patient endeavour by plant breeders, who've succeeded in producing the perfect spaghetti.'

The report continued in this light-hearted vein and came to a merry conclusion with pictures of the jolly Swiss villagers tucking into the first strands of the new crop.

After the programme the BBC was inundated by viewers' enquiries. Many were outraged that a serious current affairs programme should have been degraded in this way. But there was a sizeable number who were genuinely interested in travelling out to see the harvest the following year, and several keen to buy a few spaghetti plants to begin cultivation at home.

Regrettably, those days of innocence have more or less gone for ever. We all whizz from A to B in aeroplanes, rather as we used to in omnibuses. The world really does seem a smaller place, and almost nowhere is free from the relentless tide of modernization. Seeing some of the consequences, one can almost sympathize with Mahatma Gandhi who was once asked for his opinion of Western civilization – and replied that he thought it would be a very good idea.

There was an English businessman doing a tiring sales round for his firm in the Middle East who stopped over in Cairo for a few days to recover before flying home. One afternoon he went for a camel ride in a remote oasis. Alone, except for his Arab guide, he was filled by the romance of the barren wastes that stretched away to the horizon in every direction. For that one afternoon he was transported to the world of *Kismet* and *Beau Geste*. His ride over, he handed the guide a generous tip and asked with a distant look in his eye, 'What is my camel's name?'

'Miss Piggy,' was the reply.

Further south, Kenya has been a popular haunt of British residents and a good many visitors for much of this century. Not that long ago a holidaymaker and her husband on safari stopped to photograph a group of Masai warriors. The lady was pointing her camera in their direction when they suddenly began shouting and waving their spears at her.

'Put that camera away,' snapped her husband. 'They think you're going to trap their spirits or something inside it.'

'No, no, Mister,' said their guide. 'They only say your missus still has lens cap on.'

In a similar vein was the experience of the mobile X-ray teams that went out into the Australian bush twenty years ago as part of a mass radiography programme. Everyone was invited to take advantage of the free service, but the teams found that many aborigines, accustomed to posing for tourist cameras, were asking for modelling fees before agreeing to have their X-rays taken.

Scepticism about the real educational value of travel is strengthened by examples like that of an Englishman and an American who found themselves sharing a railway compartment one summer afternoon in central Italy. The American asked where his companion was heading.

'To Assisi,' replied the Englishman.

'Say . . . is that one of those smart resorts?' the American enquired.

'No, I very much doubt it,' said his fellow traveller a trifle disdainfully. 'I am going there to visit the birthplace of St Francis.'

'Oh, really . . . and what's so special about him?'

Realizing the genuineness of this question, the Englishman gave a thumbnail hagiography, highlighting St Francis's renunciation of wealth and possessions and his great sense of charity.

'That's a good story. He sounds quite a guy,' acknowledged the American when his companion had finished his tale.

As he was leaving the train a short while later, he shook hands with the Englishman and said, 'It's been nice talking to you. If you're ever in the States be sure to come and look me up in my birthplace.'

'And where is that?' he was asked.

'San Francisco,' he replied.

Visiting urban America is an experience like no other on earth. New York must be the only place in the world that you go out for a newspaper at night and the next morning you're in it! Where else can you rob a bank and get mugged on the way to the getaway car?

A man said to me, 'Would you like to share a taxi?'

I said, 'How kind.'

He said, 'OK, you take the hubcaps and I'll take the tyres.'

I first went to Las Vegas to make a documentary for the BBC. We were a small team and very much innocents abroad. For instance we wanted to film in a casino and after some negotiation we received permission to shoot the world's largest poker game, with me playing in it, at the Golden Horseshoe in Glitter Gulch. You can see the sort of money they make in the place in as much as they have a million dollars in notes under Perspex in front of which punters can be photographed. When you think they're losing perhaps $100,000 a year in lost interest you can see that they don't exactly have a cash-flow problem.

Las Vegas really is the most awful, disgusting, vulgar city in the whole wide world – and I love every moment of it. There are slot machines everywhere. I suppose one of the most exciting moments in my life was going to the loo in Las Vegas and hearing somebody win the jackpot in the next cubicle.

Las Vegas – they call it the city of ecology because when you leave Vegas you leave *clean*. They are, I'm told, bringing a new law into Nevada. They're sending all the hookers to the Virgin Islands to be recycled.

They say Vegas is the most religious city in the world. There are all those people walking round saying 'Oh my God! Oh my God! Oh my God!'

Down in the cheap area of Vegas, which is called Glitter Gulch, the habitués play the penny slots wearing workmen's gloves because their hands get so blistered. They wander round with large plastic cups filled with nickels. They can't keep their money in their handbags. Their handbags are filled with ashtrays.

People sit there oblivious to whether it's night or day, playing hour after hour. One of the most unusual games is

Keeno, a sort of variant of bingo. You can always spot them by the lift – they press five buttons. Then there are the chaps who have played crap all day. You can spot them as well. They'll be standing in the elevator and you say, 'Which floor do you want?'

They reply, 'Five – but it'll never come up.'

Few of the world's frontier lands can have been catapulted so headlong into the thick of the twentieth century as the American West. Travelling there a century ago was quite a different experience, as the great American impresario, Charles Frohman, discovered when, in his early days, he undertook a pioneering tour through the old cattle country of the Mid West soon after the Northern Pacific Railway had been completed. (In Mrs Patrick Campbell's words, this was very much more a case of being forced to tour than being a *tour de force*.)

One night on the way out West, the train was halted by a wrecked bridge near Miles City, Montana, and thus beleaguered it was set upon by a group of cowboys who started to shoot it up for a spot of fun. Frohman saved the situation with the timely suggestion, 'We've got a theatrical company here and we'll give you a performance.'

The cowboys agreed, and the leading man was winkled out from the safety of his compartment to stand on the prairie under the stars reciting such elevating pieces as 'The Smuggler's Life', 'The Execution' and 'The Sanguinary Pirate'. The cowboys loved it and showed their appreciation by firing their six-guns into the night sky and joining in raucously with the recitation.

The journey back East was no less eventful. Most of the scenery had to be abandoned, leaving a single backdrop showing the interior of a cathedral to provide the setting for every scene from a casino to a ballroom.

Money became so short that Frohman played in any town where there was the slightest chance of raising an audience. So they appeared in schoolhouses and barns, at times exiting with the lamps acting as footlights to use them backstage in their makeshift dressing-rooms.

By the time they had reached Bozeman, Montana, there was just $330 left in the kitty. With his company assembled in the railway booking hall, Frohman went to the ticket office and presented the clerk with their entire assets.

'Where do you want to go?' asked the clerk.

'How far will this take us?' asked Frohman, pushing the pile of money towards him.

'To Billings,' said the clerk, after a quick head count.

'Ladies and gentlemen,' said Frohman, 'we play Billings next.'

Off they set across the prarie limping from one booking to the next.

In Bismarck, North Dakota, they performed *Moths*, a play in which the slighted hero, a singer, utters the anguished line, 'There are many marquises, but very few tenors.'

In the parlous financial straits in which Frohman and company found themselves, this line had a disastrous significance and the performance virtually ground to a halt as they fell about in uncontrollable laughter; Frohman laughing louder and longer than anyone.

They were finally forced to throw in the towel at Winona, Minnesota. Frohman managed to borrow enough money to get everyone safely back to New York and before they dispersed gave them all IOUs to cover their back pay in full. To his credit every cent had been paid within five years.

Money certainly wasn't a problem when Gabriel Pascal took his company to Egypt to film scenes for Shaw's *Caesar and Cleopatra*. Worried that some of the well-known local features might not be quite up to scratch after several thousand years lying around the desert, the company took their own home-made sphinx with them: this was reckoned to be more photogenic than the real thing. When they returned to England the sphinx was left behind 'For Egypt', as Gabriel Pascal explained. To emphasize the point, he got a stonemason to engrave on it, 'With the compliments of J. Arthur Rank'.

The British have always been adept at leaving their stamp on other nations and not always in the most culturally enriching ways. There was a group of expatriates living a life of ease in sunny Marbella who nevertheless felt such a need for the familiar and homely that they opened a launderette and named it El Stanmore.

A market stall selling clothes in Italy was seen to be carrying a line of pullovers bearing the label 'Best Scottish Knitwear. Jock McPhoney. Made in Scotland.' – though admittedly their provenance was somewhat hazy.

However, there was little doubt about the clothes that were so eagerly snapped up by the good people of Kiev when a Welsh visitor decided to make a ready rouble by flogging off his outfit. His jacket went for the equivalent of forty pounds. He sold his tie for a fiver. He even sold his trousers. They fetched thirty quid. Within a short time he was down to his underwear but better off by almost a hundred pounds.

The chap who bought his trousers had assured him that he could buy another pair round the corner for under ten pounds. Unfortunately the shop was closed and it was while he was wandering about trying to find another that the Welshman was hauled in by the Kiev police on a charge of indecent exposure. That was in the days of Leonid Brezhnev; with *glasnost* sweeping through the Soviet Union he might have found the rate of exchange less favourable.

Under Mr Khrushchev visitors definitely found a more earnest approach to life. In the early 1960s a party of five young bloods drove a 1933 Rolls-Royce to Moscow and back to see what things were really like behind the Iron Curtain. In spite of petrol costing half-a-crown a gallon ('rather smelly stuff, but it worked') they found Mother Russia less than alluring. They deplored the lack of nightlife and said that most of the Russians they met seemed to spend their time reading good books.

From some accounts the situation hadn't improved measurably by the time of the Moscow Olympics in 1980. Returning to his hotel one evening, a western visitor asked one of the more approachable Intourist guides, 'Where is the nearest nightclub I can go for a meal?'

With a smile she replied, 'Helsinki.'

In contrast to this 'famine' was the 'feast' enjoyed by Somerset Maugham during a deliberately opulent holiday in which he indulged himself grandly in Spain. Since he discovered that he couldn't remove his Spanish royalties from the country, he decided that he might as well enjoy them in style. So he installed himself in one of the best hotels to wine and dine extravagantly until he had worked his way through the earnings from the Spanish editions of his works. Once he was satisfied that he and the national exchequer were just about quits he informed the manager that he would be leaving the hotel the following morning and asked for his bill.

'It's been an honour having you here,' the manager replied to his distinguished guest. 'You've brought us much valuable publicity. Therefore, there is no bill.'

The British have a way of managing to enjoy themselves abroad, often in spite of the most trying circumstances. Even a revolution failed to prevent a stalwart tourist from Yorkshire from having a good time when she stayed on the coast near Bone during the Algerian uprising. 'It's a very happy revolution,' she told reporters when she got home. 'I think the newspapers are making too much of it. It is really thrilling in Algiers and I couldn't have been more comfortable.'

They also have a knack of importing a degree of good old Blighty into the wildest and most exotic locations. Back in the last century, when Britain still played a key part in the Great Game that Kipling so loved, a surveyor beavering away high up in the remote Pamir mountains where Russia, China, Afghanistan and India (as it then was) meet, found himself a bit short of the ready. A passing yakherd was happy to help him out and in return the surveyor wrote out an IOU for twenty quid on a sheet of notepaper. Almost a year later this same piece of paper showed up at his bank, after being presented at their Peshawar branch up on the Northwest Frontier. In the intervening period it had changed hands many times. Thumb prints dotted all over showed that several of the 'bearers', to use the argot of printed currency, had been illiterate. The note had travelled far and wide across central Asia; one mark showed it had been to Samarkand. But everywhere it had been taken without question as being worth twenty pounds.

One wonders whether banking has really made any strides since then. It's obvious to one and all that poor old Sterling hasn't.

For sheer initiative I still relish the enterprise shown by the wife of a District Commissioner who took a close interest in the welfare of the 'wives' in the local emir's harem. Many of them were little more than girls when they entered the hallowed portals for life; the emir liked them young. While acknowledging that he had a beautiful home and they were well cared for, this good lady couldn't help noticing that time did hang rather heavily on their hands and some of them tended to get a bit bored.

With a breadth of imagination that could only have been nurtured in these shores she suggested to the emir that they might all become Girl Guides.

He was said to be very taken with the idea: it would give them something to do.

Duty Calls

TRAVELLING FOR PLEASURE is one thing, travelling as part of one's daily round and common toil is quite another matter and actors can find themselves suffering more than most in this respect.

I suppose the most hectic piece of travel in which I have been involved was when I managed to secure leave from the long-running London musical *Charlie Girl* to make a cowboy film, *A Talent for Loving*, with Dick Widmark in Spain. I was only allowed out on condition that I returned to England by a certain date, not just to rejoin the ranks of *Charlie Girl* but also to rehearse my *Gas and Gaiters* television series. Inevitably the film overran and the producer was in a frightful quandary because such was the plot that in no way could the film end without me. Well, as I could not possibly postpone my English commitments there was only one solution – to commute to Madrid.

So for ten horrendous days I leapt off stage at 10.15 after my nightly performance, removed my make-up in a car swishing me to London Airport, caught the 11.15 plane to Madrid and arrived at my hotel at 1.30 a.m. Each day I was on location forty kilometres outside Madrid at seven in the morning. I then caught the lunchtime plane back to London, rehearsed for *Gas and Gaiters* in the afternoon and was back on stage doing *Charlie Girl* in the evening. Actually the odd thing about it was that as the whole venture was so decidedly loopy one didn't really seem to get tired – just giggly.

That experience made me sympathize with the predicament in which G. K. Chesterton used to find himself with disquieting frequency. Chesterton was notoriously absent-minded and relied on his wife totally to take care of the practical side of his business and private life. While he was travelling around the country once on a lecture tour she received a telegram reading, 'Am in Birmingham. Where ought I to be?'

'Home,' she cabled back.

Theatrical tours can also be quite a test of one's appetite for travel. Lilian Baylis's company discovered some of the pitfalls of playing away from home when they were invited by the Danish Tourist Board to take a production of *Hamlet* to Elsinore to inaugurate an annual festival to be held in the castle there.

Their difficulties began the moment they arrived and saw that the set which had been designed by a Danish artist bore little resemblance to the designs they had sent. Work had to begin on a new one straightaway.

Then came the problem over rehearsals. No one in the tourist board had thought to tell the castle authorities that the company would need to rehearse. They refused to close its doors to tourists by day, so rehearsals had to take place at night – from midnight until six in the morning.

Although it was built almost entirely of stone, the powers that be also regarded their castle as a fire risk and insisted that a detachment of firemen should be on hand all the time in case of accidents. So night after night part of the late shift of the Elsinore brigade were treated to the sight of Miss Baylis's company going through their paces under the direction of Tyrone Guthrie.

To compound their hardships it rained most nights, saturating everyone. Miss Baylis suffered along with her troops, dispensing sandwiches and squash, and on especially vile evenings something rather stronger, in the best traditions of the WVS.

The first performance carried considerable prestige. The Danish royal family and a sizeable section of the royal court were scheduled to travel up to Elsinore by train and in their wake trooped press and media people from all over Europe.

Then the heavens really opened. Miss Baylis held a council of war half an hour before the curtain was due to go up and it was decided to scrub round the castle altogether and retire to the comfort of a hotel ballroom. Theatre in the round hadn't been invented yet, but that's what the audience experienced that night.

Lilian Baylis marshalled her troops, improvised some very hasty rehearsals to let everyone know where the entrances and exits were supposed to be, and set hands to shifting eight hundred or so chairs to accommodate the audience. While all this was going on, she donned her academic gown and hood and waded in to keep the royal party happy until everything was ready.

In the event the performance was carried off with considerable success and launched the Elsinore Festival with a certain, if rather unpredictable, style.

It might have run even more smoothly if the hotel management had been a little more accommodating in allowing all the facilities of the ballroom to be used. As it was, one pair of double doors which would have provided an ideal entrance was resolutely ruled out of bounds. The reason for this was explained the following morning.

The head porter cautiously indicated a tiny nest above the outer face of the doors, where a pair of blue tits were bringing their little feathered brood into the world. If the door had been opened, he explained, the mother would have abandoned the nest and that would never have done. (Look what happened to Hamlet, after all.)

For some ten years now, we've been presenting plays in Kuala Lumpur. One night the King of Malaysia, the Yang di-Pertuan Agong, booked the whole theatre for his own private guests, it being the Malaysian National Army Day. The play we were performing was Noël Coward's *Blithe Spirit* and it starred Peggy Mount, Paula Wilcox and John Stride. It was a splendid production and one of which I was very proud.

I was a little alarmed, however, when I went into the auditorium that evening: the king had brought a full military band to play for him while he was dining before the show. But more of a worry to me was a large platform, rather higher than the stage that had been erected for us, upon which sat the king and the Raja Permasuri Agong, together with assorted generals, various tunkus and other officials. The rest of the audience were seated behind this platform and it was obvious to me that when the play commenced there was no way in which they would be able to see it. It would also be exceedingly alarming for the actors when the play opened to find this bethroned assembly rising high above them a mere three or four feet away. What was I to do?

Fortunately, at the end of the meal and before the play started, the king was invited to go to the loo. Now, being a monarch, he couldn't go to an ordinary mortal's loo, so he was taken to a suitably grand throne room on the thirtieth floor of the building in which we were performing.

I acted swiftly. With the help of a couple of generals and members of the military band, we quickly removed the platform and the various thrones, spread a deal of red carpeting on the floor and put upon it two very comfortable armchairs, one for the king, the other for the queen. And there between the seats, and this was the *pièce de résistance*, we placed a magnum of Dom Pérignon.

When the royal party returned they looked decidedly grumpy at first that the thrones had disappeared. But soon they espied the exceedingly comfortable armchairs and more particularly the chilled bottle waiting invitingly between them.

Sir Thomas Beecham once took the LPO to Brussels to give a concert containing a fair proportion of English music. As a consequence the orchestra received a government subsidy, the first in fact that had ever been paid. On their arrival, however, it was discovered that the case with all the music had been mislaid on landing at Ostend.

From the library of the Salle des Beaux Arts they were able to lay their hands on Beethoven's fifth symphony, a symphony by Haydn and a Mendelssohn overture and made do with these.

But it was left to Beecham to explain to his Belgian audience, 'At long last His Majesty's Government have recognized the existence of British music by supporting this visit to Brussels, but we are unfortunately unable to play any of it owing to an oversight on the part of Belgian Railways.'

Tel Aviv boasts the impressive Mann auditorium which is on the itinerary of most VIPs who visit the city. It was certainly on the list of places that the former West German chancellor, Willy Brandt, was taken to during an official visit he made while serving as mayor of West Berlin. He looked suitably impressed by the famous concert hall and expressed his special appreciation that the Israelis had thought fit to name it after the great German writer Thomas Mann. Here he was interrupted by his host who politely corrected him. The hall had actually been named after one Frederic Mann of Philadelphia.

'What ever did he write?' asked Willy Brandt in amazement.

'A cheque,' was the reply.

Keeping your wits about you is one of the essentials of official visits, as many a politician has discovered to his cost. Gerald Ford once found himself called on to propose a toast during a banquet held in his honour by the former Egyptian president Anwar Sadat. Raising his glass the leader of the western world announced, 'To the great people and the Government of Israel . . . excuse me, of Egypt.'

In May 1981 the recently appointed South African ambassador to Uruguay gave his first press conference in Montevideo and told the assembled journalists, 'I am very happy to be in Peru.'

During the last war, when several of the crowned heads of Europe had sought refuge in these shores, King Haakon of Norway made broadcasts from time to time to his people suffering under the Nazi jackboot. On one occasion he turned up at Bush House when he should have gone to Broadcasting House. As a result there was no one waiting at reception to meet him.

'I am the King of Norway,' he told the commissionaire on duty, who then set about ringing round the building to try and find someone higher up the pecking order to come and sort things out. He made a number of calls without success and clearly a little harassed by the experience broke off in the middle of one conversation to ask, 'Er, 'scuse me, but where did you say you was king of?'

Some years later the corporation was thrown into another tizzy by one of King Haakon's subjects, the anthropologist Thor Heyerdahl. He was in London for a brief stopover and with a tight timetable found himself finishing a programme for ITV and going straight round to the Television Centre to record one for the BBC. To save time, the BBC producer had arranged to send a taxi to collect him directly from the ITV studio, but as he waited in the reception area and no taxi appeared the master of the *Kon-Tiki* began to grow anxious. In the end he spotted a man who looked as if he might be a taxi driver and seemed to be searching for someone himself and asked, 'Excuse me, I'm Thor Heyerdahl. Are you looking for me?'

'No mate,' said the taxi driver. 'I've been sent to pick up four Airedales for the BBC.'

The talkative wife of an English MP suffered equal confusion when she took her seat at a banquet next to a Chinese gentleman. Assuming that his lack of conversation was due to a limited knowledge of English rather than her ceaseless monologue, she switched to an improvised pidgin English, which from his smiles and nods he appeared to understand.

She was still chatting away vivaciously when the toastmaster 'prayed silence' for his Excellency the Chinese Ambassador. To her amazement the man to whom she had been talking rose to his feet and delivered the most polished and amusing after-dinner speech in perfect English.

As the enthusiastic applause was dying away at its close Dr Wellington Koo whispered in his neighbour's ear, 'Likee speechee?'

Last year I was at a small dinner party with the then Chinese ambassador to London. Sitting next to his wife was Michael Heseltine. The conversation turned to the immense variety of Chinese regional food now available in London: Sichuan, Shanghaiese, Pekingese, Cantonese etc. Eventually Michael asked, 'Now, madam, where do you like to eat in London?'

We all waited. Would it be Ken Low's Memories of China, Mr Chow, or perhaps Poon's?

'What I like best, Mr Heseltine,' replied the ambassador's wife, 'is English fish and chips out of a newspaper.'

British guests of a wildly eccentric Indian maharajah before partition found him to be of a very generous nature when it came to extending hospitality. He obeyed no prohibitions against alcohol, and even went to the extent of installing a model railway on his banqueting table to carry port to his guests after dinner. This simple device gave him the most enormous pleasure. The controls were placed by his seat at the head of the table and he used to take an almost childish delight in speeding up the little locomotive just as an unwitting guest was reaching for the decanter, leaving him grasping desperately after it as it hurtled down the track.

Even in the 'old Commonwealth' British visitors can be caught out by local customs they don't find at home. When Prince Charles spent a couple of terms during his schooldays at Timbertop in Australia he went to church one Sunday morning and found the pews very thinly populated. As he left after the service the rector apologized that there hadn't been more of the congregation to keep him company. It was a bank holiday weekend, he explained, and most of the parishioners were away.

'Not another bank holiday,' said his royal visitor. 'What's this one in aid of?'

'Well, over here,' replied the rector, rather awkwardly, 'we call it the Queen's Birthday.'

The royal family must undertake more 'business' travel than many of the boards of directors of major corporations put together and what makes their ordeal all the more demanding is that they can't arrive at an airport tired and frowsty but conveniently cloaked in anonymity.

Some time ago the Duke of Edinburgh flew to a provincial airport to attend an official engagement nearby. At the foot of the steps from the plane he was met by a reception committee whose leader was obviously a little overawed by the occasion. Thinking of nothing better to say, he asked what the flight had been like.

'Have you ever flown in a plane?' asked the Duke.

'Oh, yes, your Royal Highness, several times.'

'Well, it was just like that.'

Those airport meetings and interviews are always pretty dreadful. One is tired and feeling more dreary than usual, to be faced with the inevitable question, 'So Mr Nimmo, what do you think of Melbourne/New York/Cape Town' or wherever.

One is always tempted to reply, 'Well, the roofs look very nice.'

It is so easy to find yourself hugely misquoted at times; like Lord Fisher, when Archbishop of Canterbury, preparing to visit the United States for the first time. He was duly warned of the insidious approaches of the press and was determined to meet them with aloofness and dignity. Confronted by a barrage of cameras and newsmen as he disembarked, he answered the flippant question, 'Do you intend to visit any nightclubs during your stay, my lord?' with cold and lordly sarcasm.

'*Are* there any nightclubs in New York?'

The next morning the headline in the press blazed out, 'ARCHBISHOP'S FIRST QUESTION ON UNITED STATES SOIL: "ARE THERE ANY NIGHTCLUBS IN NEW YORK?"'

(Churchill left his opinion until he was safely home on this side of the Atlantic. Asked what he'd thought of New York, he muttered, 'Newspapers too thick. Lavatory paper too thin.')

Archbishops have a tough time at airports in general, it would appear from an outraged letter sent by the editor of Debrett's to *The Times* ten years ago. He expressed his astonishment that the late Lord Ramsey, who until four years earlier had been Archbishop of Canterbury and second only to the Royal Family in the order of precedence, should not have been eligible to use the VIP lounges at Heathrow. Who was granted VIP status by the British Airports Authority, he wanted to know, 'some television "personalities" and some entertainers?' I wonder.

Mind you, perhaps Lord Ramsey would have liked to have been an entertainer himself. While he was still Archbishop, I received one morning a telephone call from Lambeth Palace. It was the Primate of All England himself. 'I wonder whether you would agree to appear with me on a stage at the Southern Agricultural Show?' he asked.

For a moment I had wild thoughts of our becoming an ecclesiastical counterpart to Morecombe and Wise. But no. 'I thought we could just have a little conversation about Christianity,' he continued.

Sadly I was doing something else that particular Saturday, so I shall never know how it might have turned out.

In the normal line of their 'work' bishops as a rule regard themselves as anything but VIPs and I'm sure that Dr Ramsey was far less concerned about his status at Heathrow than many others scrabbling to make the most of whatever perks their plane tickets accorded them. His successor, Dr Coggan, went on a 'meet the people' campaign during his time as Archbishop of York and one evening took a train from there – riding on the footplate. As it was a normal business trip, however, he insisted on paying his normal first-class fare.

William Cecil, sometime Bishop of Exeter, evidently felt less at ease travelling by train. He was extraordinarily absent-minded and travelling once to a confirmation service he mislaid his ticket and simply couldn't find it when the ticket collector came to inspect it.

'That's all right, my lord,' the collector assured him, 'we know who you are.'

'That's as may be,' replied the bishop, 'but without my ticket how am I to know where I am going?'

Over the water in Canada many years ago a recently appointed Governor General knew only too well where he was going but was stymied by unforeseen circumstances. As his train chuffed into the station at Ottawa on a crisp morning in the middle of winter and came to a halt alongside the red carpet, aides jumped out, the guard of honour snapped to attention and the band prepared to play the National Anthem. A pause followed which slowly lengthened into an embarrassing delay. Meanwhile, inside the Governor General's carriage, he was struggling in his bathroom. Cold as he knew Canada to be, he hadn't reckoned on the water in his tooth mug freezing solid. But it had, trapping his false teeth inside.

The Duke of Windsor was another British 'administrator' who experienced some difficulty in getting used to daily life in North America – and just about anywhere else, for that matter. In spite of becoming Governor of the Bahamas during the war, he never really grasped the fundamentals that apply to most other people. For a month in 1943 he and the Duchess spent a glorious holiday in the pampered ease of The Homestead, a luxurious hotel in Hot Springs, Virginia. As they were getting ready for their departure the Duke was presented with their bill. He took it uncomprehendingly and muttered, 'Now what do I do with this?' – and from all accounts that was the end of the matter. They left The Homestead with the bill unpaid.

During one of the downturns in American fortunes in the Vietnam War, President Johnson suggested that it might be good for morale if he gave a few words of personal encouragement to the troops before they flew out to Indo-China to do their bit for the free world.

The Pentagon agreed to this, so did the White House staff. The only ones who seemed less than enthusiastic were the troops themselves, most of whom were so thoroughly depressed at the prospect of fighting in Vietnam that they had resorted to Dutch courage and were in no state to meet anyone, let alone their President when he stepped out of Air Force One to wish them goodbye.

It fell to the PR people to rescue the situation and, with inspiration born of the moment, the boys about to be flown out to Vietnam were replaced by a plane-load who had just returned from completing their tour of duty.

They were in high good spirits and the President was so

heartened by them that he insisted on staying to wave their plane goodbye as it took off!

Further hasty arrangements were made. The bemused troops were herded back on to the plane in which they had just landed to fly round in circles until the presidential jet itself had taken off and was well out of sight.

In days gone by the correspondents sent out to cover wars around the world used to find themselves at rather a loose end at times. There's the celebrated story of the artist Frederic Remington who was sent to Cuba by the newspaper proprietor William Randolph Hearst after the American battleship *Maine* had been blown up in Havana harbour early in 1898. Hearst had anticipated immediate war with Cuba and wanted pictures from the front, but no war resulted. Remington sent a cable asking whether he should come.

'Please remain,' Hearst cabled back. 'You furnish the pictures and I'll furnish the war.'

Fourteen years later war broke out in the Balkans and *The Times* sent Maurice Baring to cover the conflict. The fighting was sporadic, however, and having time on his hands with nothing else to do Baring interspersed his war reports with theatrical notices and commentaries on Eastern literature.

Thirty years ago a Queen's Messenger and his guard found themselves in the same part of the world, travelling by train from Vienna to Bucharest. It was Christmas Day and, refusing to allow the atheistic chill of their Communist surroundings to dull their seasonal spirits, they kitted themselves out with appropriately festive accoutrements. In the compartment they installed a camping stove and pressure cooker to prepare their turkey and plum pudding. While this was bubbling away they busied themselves with holly, mistletoe and paper streamers brought along to jolly up the carriage.

During the war the US ambassador in Moscow became accustomed to being shadowed everywhere he went by the KGB. So it was that one winter weekend he let it be known that he was going to visit a British diplomat in the countryside outside Moscow. The ambassador also hinted to the secret police that his host's retreat could only be reached by four-wheel-drive vehicles, but in spite of this considerate warning his jeep was followed by the same type of saloon car that habitually shadowed him. This kept up until they left the metalled road, at which point the KGB vehicle was soon bogged down. A solitary secret policeman then left the comfort of the car and set off on foot to follow the American ambassador. He in turn asked his driver to slow down, so that the policeman wasn't left behind. But after a while he became seriously concerned that the man might get frostbite if he stayed in the open much longer and, promising that he wouldn't tell a soul, offered the KGB man a lift. This he accepted and pursuer and pursued drove along together until they reached their destination – adding a new dimension to what was to become the cold war.

Few diplomatic remarks can top that of a very junior secretary at his first embassy party who was nervously chatting to a senior member of the East German delegation when he was asked, 'Have you ever visited Berlin?'

'No, I'm afraid I haven't,' replied the young man, 'but my father flew over it during the war.'

Up, Up, and Away

I'M SURE THAT there must be a good many travellers who share the view of Al Boliska that 'Airline travel is hours of boredom interrupted by moments of stark terror,' but in spite of a few close shaves I can't honestly count myself among their number.

I am, to be truthful, the travel agent's dream. A completely hooked, no chance of a cure travelholic. People say to me continually, 'How can you possibly enjoy living out of suitcases?' Well, I adore it. To me the most beautiful smell in the world is that of a jet engine revving up on sunbaked tarmac.

Immediately the adrenalin starts to flow, my senses are alive, and my whole body tingling with anticipation.

Travel is, I suppose a basic instinct, but nothing has changed the face of modern travel more radically than the big jet aircraft. Today everything and everywhere is possible. Now, thanks to the big jets, you can have your breakfast in London, lunch in New York, dinner in Los Angeles . . . and all of this while your luggage is on its way to Buenos Aires.

Luckily I have never been remotely afraid of flying, but for the nervous it always seems to me a trifle insensitive that the first sign they see when they reach the airport reads 'Terminal'. One feels their point of departure could be labelled more hopefully. For me, however, the longer the journey the better. What I absolutely love about the long intercontinental routes is the feeling of complete irresponsibility and self-indulgence. Once the plane has zoomed into the sky there is nothing one has to do but enjoy oneself. Nobody can telephone. One is totally cut off from everyday life. There is absolutely no feeling of guilt as one eats, drinks, reads or watches the film. One enters into a pampered make-believe world which anaesthetizes the world's problems for a blissful umpteen hours; literally as near to heaven as one will get above this earth.

It's such a pity that the experience of flying hasn't always been like this.

Of course the mistake that so many air travellers have made is undertaking the actual process of flying themselves. The freedom enjoyed aloft by the birds is best left to them in my opinion; leave me to the gin and tonic and my headset.

There was poor Oliver of Malmesbury, a Benedictine monk of the eleventh century who let notions of flying under his own power leap wildly beyond reason. Strapping a pair of home-made wings to his hands and feet one day, he launched himself from the turret of a lofty tower and into the arms of his Maker. Oliver wasn't the first (or the last) to discover that when the Good Lord gave man 'dominion' over the 'fowl of the air' he didn't intend us to be up there exercising it alongside them.

It was a literal case of 'fowl of the air' that did for the aviation exploits of the late fifteenth-century Abbot of Tongland, John Damian. Taking a break from his usual scientific interest in alchemy, for which James IV of Scotland paid him good money to try to turn base metals into gold, he also kitted himself out with a pair of wings made from birds' feathers and threw himself off the ramparts of Stirling Castle. He was luckier than Oliver of Malmesbury and escaped with nothing graver than a broken thigh and a rather grimy habit, having landed in the castle's dung-heap.

In this he saw the flaw in his design. Having made the mistake of using hens' feathers, he argued, his wings were naturally attracted towards the dung-heap, where hens spent much of their time. If he'd used eagles' feathers, who knows how far he might have soared. As it was, he was content to hobble back to his lab and get on with trying to make gold.

The early days of ballooning weren't a lot safer. Jean Pierre Blanchard, one of the French pioneers of balloon flight in the late 1700s, started out by inventing a *vaisseau volant*, a 'flying vessel' fitted with four wings worked by two pedals and two hand levers. In spite of his claims that he had managed to raise it off the ground, no one else ever witnessed a flight and he soon turned his creative powers to the recently invented balloons. He tried fitting these with rowing wings, but on his first ascent over the Champs de Mars in Paris a gentle wind obstinately blew him in one direction while he tried rowing frantically the other way: the wings went back to the drawing-board and Blanchard set off for England to seek his fortune as an aviator.

There a well-orchestrated publicity campaign attracted the attention of several well-heeled backers, among them Dr John Jeffries, an American living in London, with whom Blanchard planned the first aerial crossing of the Channel. After a considerable amount of chicanery in which Blanchard tried various ways of ditching Jeffries once his money had been spent equipping the flight, including wearing a lead belt under his shirt and claiming at the last minute that the balloon was overweight, the ill-starred duo cast off from Dover Castle and were wafted out over the sea towards France.

Their troubles began less than ten miles from the English coast when the balloon began losing height and since neither of them could swim they chucked cargo over the side for all they were worth. The next crisis struck soon after they spotted the French coast and this time Blanchard flung away all but his underwear as they sank towards the wave tops. The fact that they were crossing in early January may have had something to do with his companion's refusal to discard his clothing, maintaining that he'd rather drown than face the French in the nude. But with their basket dipping into the whitecaps, he too jettisoned his clothes. When even more weight had to be lost they climbed into the rigging and discharged their bladders into the English Channel.

Not long after, a further calamity struck when warm wind blowing offshore lifted them skywards. The anchors and landing ropes had gone over the side in the first panic, so with no means of bringing themselves earthwards the first men to cross the Channel by air drifted forlornly over the Pas de Calais, decidedly chilly by this stage. Above the Forest of Guines Jeffries managed to slow their progress by grabbing passing treetops and in the nick of time a clearing emerged into which Blanchard was able to drop the balloon with a judicious release of its gas. His conquest was rewarded with a handsome bequest from Louis XVI and a lifetime pension. Dr Jeffries didn't get a penny.

Tranquil and effortless as it looks, ballooning isn't without hazards for the uninitiated. Seventy years after Blanchard's epic flight, a couple of his fellow countrymen enjoying a sunny afternoon in Cannes took it into their heads to go for a spin with a balloonist from Nice who'd invited them to join him. They'd taken their seats in the basket and were waiting for the 'pilot' to climb in, when a voice from the crowd called out in excitement, 'Let go.' The men holding the anchor ropes obeyed the command and, in the words of *The Times* correspondent who witnessed the incident, 'the balloon rose rapidly into the clouds and disappeared'. As both passengers were 'entirely ignorant of the management of a balloon' their chances looked slim and, as the man from *The Times* laconically reported, 'Up to the 2nd no intelligence of them had been received.'

From more recent times comes the tale of a pair of young lovers from Nevada who climbed into what they thought was a large crate one dark and balmy night and only discovered some hours later when a violent storm blew out of the desert that it was the gondola of a balloon, which duly broke from its moorings. For them the earth more than moved that night.

The sport of gliding has had few more enthusiastic followers than Sir George Cayley of Brompton Hall, in Yorkshire. He is credited with designing and building the first working glider in 1852 though, in the finest tradition of the landed gentry, left the piloting of its maiden flight the following year to his coachman. This poor chap was inveigled into the contraption on one side of a small valley near Brompton Hall and launched across to the other side rather like a giant balsa-wood toy. Fortunately his master's grasp of aerodynamics ensured that he landed reasonably safely, though as soon as the excited inventor had panted to within earshot, the coachman's first words were, 'Please, Sir

George, I wish to give notice. I was hired to drive, not fly.'
Quite so.

When it came to powered flight, uncertainty and scepticism
reigned even in the most erudite scientific circles. Lord
Kelvin, President of the Royal Society in the early 1890s,
commented that 'Heavier than air [flying] machines are im-
possible.' Across the Atlantic his opinion was shared by the
eminent astronomer Simon Newcomb who, among other
posts, was in charge of the Naval Observatory in Washington.
'Aerial flight is one of the class of problems with which man
will never be able to cope,' he avowed. Unfortunately Orville
and Wilbur Wright down on their windy beach at Kitty Hawk
missed this pronouncement and quietly got on with building
and flying the first real aeroplane.

In some respects Newcomb was right about the problems
'aerial flight' was likely to provoke. Anyone living under the
Heathrow flight path will have a word or two to say on the
subject. So will air traffic controllers just about anywhere in
the world. And so did HM Collector of Customs at Dover
when another Frenchman scored a flying first by crossing the
English Channel by plane one morning in July 1909.

> 'Hon Sirs,' began the report, 'I have to report that M.
> Blériot, with his monoplane, successfully crossed the
> Channel from Calais this morning.
>   . . . I visited the spot where he landed at 6.30 a.m.,
> and got into conversation with an individual largely
> interested in the Wright aeroplane who gave it as his
> opinion that although airships will never come into com-
> mercial use, there are great possibilities in store for them,
> and I think that a time may come when this Department
> will have to treat their arrival seriously.'

(Try queuing in the Customs Hall at Gatwick any holiday
weekend to learn the wisdom of his prophecy.)

A fellow customs officer had found Blériot tucking into a
celebratory breakfast in a nearby pub, exhilarated at carving
a small niche for himself in the tree of scientific progress and

Travelling in style on the Orient Express   (*Chris Perkin/Orient Express*)

Backstage in London with Dame Anna Neagle (*Don Smith/Radio Times/Rennie Ellis*)

On location Down Under

In the footsteps of Captain Cook
on the Gold Coast, Australia

Fish not totally out of water
in Surfers' Paradise

'G'day, mate!' In France my interest in wine has led to my becoming a *Chevalier du vin*.
My interest in Australians has resulted in my becoming a mate of Milawa (pictured here)

(*Above left*) At the controls before buzzing the sheep and avoiding the rabbit holes . . .

(*Above right*) The art of elegant travel— by Moira Lister

(*Left*) Enjoying a drop of local juice on Australia's Great Barrier Reef

possibly more relieved at winning the £1,000 prize offered to
the first man to make the Channel flight. Having spent six
years and a sizeable fortune developing his aircraft, Blériot
wasn't exactly loaded. Indeed, he was so desperate to get his
hands on the money that he'd undertaken the flight only a
short time after the latest in his tally of fifty crashes, hobbling
on a badly burned leg and with his crutches strapped to the
fuselage.

Once on English soil he was issued with a quarantine
certificate, which designated his plane as a yacht, and Blériot
as master and owner. So began the great age of international
flight to which I have already made reference.

There is still something of that pioneering spirit about
flying even today and nowhere is it more evident than when
one moves about Australia. On one of my visits I flew a
Cessna to a country race meeting in the Northern Territory.
It took place in the Harts Range some 150 miles due east of
Alice Springs.

As I was about to land, I radioed to the control at Marakan
airport to see if there were any special landing instructions.
Back came the advice, 'Fly over first and buzz at the sheep,
and mind the rabbit holes on the right-hand side.' Rather
different from landing at Kennedy, Heathrow or Kingsford
Smith. Though not far removed, I gather from one report,
to hazards one may encounter at Nairobi, where a British
Airways 747 jumbo jet with 379 people on board had to
make an emergency landing after hitting a hyena on take-
off.

It was from Los Angeles that I departed on my first trip
in one of the original jumbos. It was a great novelty then
that there were what almost amounted to different rooms
within the plane. As I checked in at the desk the fellow
asked, 'Do you want a smoker or a non-smoking section?'

I said non-smoking.

He then asked, 'Would you like to see a clean movie or a
dirty movie?'

I hesitated, but as he obviously thought I was a bit wet, I
said firmly, 'A dirty movie.'

'Just hang on a minute,' he said, picking up the phone. 'Hey, Chuck, there's a guy here who's a non-smoker and he wants to see a dirty movie.'

There was a pause while Chuck pondered. A decision was made.

'I'm sorry, sir,' said the check-in clerk, 'you can only see the dirty movie if you're a smoker.'

One had to have two vices for the price of one! I sat in the smoker, which was bad enough, but even worse, when the film started I discovered I had already seen it.

One particular plane journey didn't especially please my wife. This took place on my twenty-fifth wedding anniversary. Unfortunately business required me to fly to the island of Bahrain on the day in question. I bade farewell to my wife at Heathrow and sat down to await take-off. She was, not to put too fine a point on it, fairly miffed. To my surprise, however, I was greeted by the chap sitting next to me with a cheery smile. 'Hello,' he said, 'how are you?'

'Frightfully well,' I replied.

'You don't remember me,' said he.

'No, I'm afraid I don't.'

'Well, there's no reason why you should.'

'Who are you?' I asked.

'Well,' he said, 'I was a choirboy at your wedding.'

'Good Lord,' said I, looking at my watch, 'it's exactly three o'clock. Twenty-five years ago to the minute you were singing "Jesu, Joy of Man's Desiring" at my wedding at Mossley Hill Church, Liverpool.'

I called a passing steward and ordered a bottle of champagne. And I sat there with my travelling companion toasting the absent wife. I certainly thought, however, that if one of the more scurrilous English newspapers had got hold of the story the headline might have read, 'NIMMO LEAVES WIFE ON TWENTY-FIFTH WEDDING ANNIVERSARY. FLIES EAST WITH FORMER CHOIRBOY'.

From some accounts enjoying a drop of your favourite tipple in flight isn't always as easy as advertisements might lead one to believe. There are stories of harassed flight attendants, trying to serve meals to planes full of recalcitrant travellers, telling passengers that water isn't available in economy class. I heard of one chap flying back from a day-long business trip to the Continent who pressed his buzzer to ask for a welcome gin and tonic only to be told that the buzzer was to be used exclusively for emergency use. Another *bon viveur* flying with our national carrier and doing it in some style, generously offered to help a stewardess who was struggling with the cork of his champagne bottle. 'I suppose you're an expert,' she replied, dismissing his gesture. As it happened he was and he told her, 'Actually I'm a Chevalier of the champagne order.'

'Yes,' she parried, still wrestling with the cork, 'but I'm insured if I put out a passenger's eye with the cork – and you're not.'

There's something about airline flight attendants that brooks no argument. Maybe it's the uniform or the fact that we're sitting while they're standing up. Even the usually vociferous Muhammad Ali was silenced by a stewardess as he was about to take off on one flight in the States. Just as the plane was taxiing to the end of the runway the stewardess reminded him to fasten his seatbelt. 'Superman don't need no seatbelt,' replied Ali.

'Superman don't need no plane either,' she retorted. The world heavyweight boxing champion duly strapped himself in.

This admirable resourcefulness is shown on the ground too. For instance there's the suitably racy episode of one BA pilot, married but secretly sharing his off-duty time and his London flat with a charming stewardess, who tired of the relationship after a year and gave his lady love her marching orders just before leaving for a stint in the Far East. She asked for a day or two to gather together her bits and pieces and when he returned a fortnight later she had gone, leaving the flat immaculately clean and tidy. The only thing out of place was the telephone receiver which had been left off the hook. The pilot picked it up to replace it and heard an American voice telling him the time – again and again at regular intervals. Before leaving, his girlfriend had dialled the speaking clock in San Francisco and his next quarterly telephone bill gave some indication of her feelings towards him.

It's the romance of travel that no doubt lends airline staff a special aura – plus the undeniable fact that many of them are also very attractive. I've always been charmed by the story of the elderly businessman about to settle down on a night flight who'd been served a drink by a very pretty stewardess and suddenly found himself saying aloud the previously unspoken thought, 'Where have you been all my life?'

The object of his desire evidently overheard this, for she smiled back and replied, 'Well, I don't really know, sir, but I guess for about two thirds of it I hadn't even been born.'

A rather more prosaic commentator in *Time and Tide* had another explanation for the popularity of British steward-esses, explaining, 'The American craze for British air host-esses is not based entirely on sentiment. Our girls tend to have shorter legs and smaller bosoms which make it easier for them to move about in a crowded plane.'

Laker Airways made more specific requirements when advertising for suitable staff for their Skytrain. They wanted girls aged between nineteen and twenty-eight, from five feet four to five feet eight inches tall, educated to GCE level, preferably with one foreign language, no spectacles and, perhaps most significantly, an ability to swim.

United Airlines were the first to employ flight attendants. This suggestion had come from the girl who turned out to be the world's first stewardess. She had written to them only a couple of months before her maiden flight in May 1930 suggesting that young ladies with appropriate qualifications might be taken on to look after the passengers; as well as being a registered nurse Ellen Church was also a private pilot. United Airlines liked the idea and not only hired her as their first stewardess, but asked her to recruit and train seven other girls for the same duties. Their job specification makes interesting reading.

Successful candidates had to be registered nurses aged twenty-five or under, weighing no more than 115 pounds and not exceeding five feet four in height. Their duties included helping the pilot and mechanics to push the aircraft in and out of the hangars, cleaning its interior, carrying the passengers' baggage and wielding a refuelling hose. At each of the stop-overs Miss Church and her colleagues collected the passengers' tickets and once they were airborne served unrelenting meals of fruit cocktail and fried chicken and rolls, washed down with tea and coffee. In return for this they were rewarded with a monthly salary of $125 and the questionable pleasure of spending a hundred hours a month aloft in an unheated and unpressurized aeroplane.

Six years later, almost to the day, nineteen-year-old Daphne Kearley took to the skies flying on the Air Dispatch 'Dawn Express' from Croydon to Le Bourget. As Britain's first stewardess she found herself required to mix cocktails, cook, speak French and type business letters that passengers would dictate to her *en route*. Actually the cooking didn't come to much because most of the time the airline provided snacks and caviar and smoked salmon. With these and the cocktails, and possibly the fact that she was Britain's one and only air stewardess before the war, Daphne found herself kept busy fending off amorous businessmen. One newspaper claimed that she'd had 299 airborne proposals in just ten months. This she denied, while admitting with admirable candour, 'It was amazing the number of men who wanted to marry me when they were flying high.'

'In America,' observed the great *New Yorker* columnist, Robert Benchley, 'there are two classes of travel – first class and with children.' The same holds true on aircraft, leading one exasperated stewardess to suggest to a little boy running up and down the gangways on a long-haul flight to Chicago, 'Look, darling, why don't you go *outside* to play?'

Then there are the hijackers, who more often than not come off the worst in their escapades. The very first aerial hijack ended in disaster for the group of Chinese bandits who tried to seize control of a Cathay Pacific flying boat shortly after it had taken off from Macao bound for Hong Kong. They had ideas of ransoming the passengers, but when the pilot resisted, they started shooting and the aircraft crashed into the sea killing everyone on board except for the hijack leader, Wong-yu Man. Rescuers took him to Hong Kong where he was placed in a hospital bed next to a police informer who had been equipped with a tape-recorder after the bullet-riddled aircraft had been salvaged. In the course of chatting to his fellow 'patient' the hijacker inadvertently gave away all the details the police needed to pin their charges on him.

Not all hijackers are blessed with a total clarity of purpose, or so it would seem judging from the behaviour of an un-identified man who drew a handgun during a flight in the USA, left his seat and grabbed as hostage one of the steward-esses, demanding to be flown to Detroit.

'But we're already going to Detroit,' she told him.

'Oh . . . good,' he answered, sitting down again.

It was in an attempt to curb this sort of air piracy that one enterprising airline engaged a couple of psychiatrists to act as special security men, with the task of arresting anyone showing signs of mental instability. Their one and only arrest was made a matter of minutes after they went on duty for the first time, when one psychiatrist apprehended the other.

On another internal flight in the USA an anxious female passenger whispered to the stewardess that she'd overheard a man muttering in a nearby seat and was sure he was a terrorist. Security forces were alerted at their destination and, when the cabin door opened, heavily armed police burst in and arrested a man identified by the stewardess's hysterical cry, 'That's the one.'

This came as rather a surprise to the gentleman at whom she pointed, an actor who'd spent the flight learning lines for his next part. But the control tower had been radioed that a hijacker was on board talking in a low voice about slavery, freedom and the overthrowing of bad government, how could he explain that? He showed them his script and they had to let him go, slightly abashed when they saw the revolutionary tract he was learning. It usually goes by the name of the Declaration of Independence.

It's experiences like this that must give airline staff a rather jaundiced view of their passengers. An elderly lady waiting to leave on a flight from Manchester asked at an enquiry desk why it had been delayed and whispered in passing that this was her first time in an aeroplane. 'There's been a crew change, madam,' she was told.

'There you are, dear,' she was heard saying to her husband. 'We change at Crewe.'

From the other side of the Atlantic came the enquiry of a passenger flying home from London to Boston who, hearing that a 'high tea' was about to be served, asked whether that had anything to do with the altitude they had reached.

Airline reservations are another constant source of annoyance, though few examples of misplaced priorities can top the case of a British scientist flying to Washington to give a lecture in the closing stages of the last war. At one of the stop-overs he was off-loaded to make room for a staff colonel who was given precedence. Realizing that he couldn't arrive in time, the scientist cancelled his lecture and caught the next plane home. Only later did it come to light that the colonel had flown to Washington with the express purpose of attending the scientist's lecture.

Some routes are less frequented than others. When British Airways started its twice-weekly Concorde service to Bahrain, the first flight took off without a single passenger on board. Asked to comment, a BA spokesman said, 'We never expected this service to be overcrowded.'

The one to New York is a different story and one British passenger, filled with national pride at its obvious excellence and commercial success, was moved to take a particularly close interest in the models of the supersonic aircraft on sale in the Concorde lounge at Kennedy airport. That's until he looked under the tailplane and found printed the words 'Made in Japan'.

Airports themselves can harbour a number of unexpected hazards, as Michael Murphy from Stevenage discovered after he'd waited in the luggage hall to reclaim the bicycle that in the last two years had carried him a distance of 25,000 miles round the world. With a bare forty miles lying between him and home, there seemed to be nothing to prevent a triumphant two-wheeled return to Stevenage. Then his bicycle appeared – crushed and twisted beyond redemption by the baggage conveyor from the plane. This left him with no option but to trudge disconsolately to the access road and start thumbing a lift.

Whilst playing Adelaide two or three years ago I was given a splendid case of Penfolds Grange Hermitage, possibly the greatest wine to come out of South Australia. This travelled with me to Hobart, Launceston, back across the water to Canberra, on to Perth, before journeying to Singapore, Bahrain and Dubai. Thirsty but expectant I waited in the baggage hall at Terminal Three at Heathrow. The first item to appear on the carousel was my collapsed box surrounded by a lake of red. Only two bottles survived.

Getting home on the cheap lay at the forefront of the mind of another young man discovered packed inside a wooden crate in the air freight terminal at Kennedy airport. He hadn't been able to afford the single fare back to Australia, he told airport officials, who'd heard him shouting for flight information from inside the container, and decided to ship himself back in the cargo hold for a tenth of the price. Two friends had nailed him into his box measuring five feet four by three feet and labelled as scientific equipment to be delivered to a laboratory in Melbourne. In there he had waited for twenty-four hours with two suitcases, a gallon of water, sandwiches, cigarettes, a large jar of air sickness pills and a stack of *Playboy* magazines to while away the long flight down under. But when there was no sign of being loaded on to a plane, he broke his silence and gave a passing cargo handler the fright of his life.

Occasionally bits and pieces of aircraft drop off while they're in flight and sometimes these aren't the most savoury substances. One morning a colossal lump of ice fell from the heavens and thudded into the lawn of a house in Surrey. This was retrieved by the police who kept it in their freezer until it was identified as a block of frozen urine, presumably jettisoned from an aircraft passing overhead. As a police spokesman later remarked, 'What with the number of aircraft about, we're very lucky it wasn't something worse.'

This was a sentiment echoed in rather more trenchant terms by a householder in the States whose home, lying directly beneath a busy flight path, was regularly bombarded by an unidentified but highly questionable material. Suspecting the worst, he complained to the Federal Aviation Administration who advised him to keep a constant watch for passing planes and note the registration number of any offending airliner.

This wasn't the course of action he had anticipated and, declining the suggestion, he told reporters, 'If they think I'm going to stand outside with my face to the sky, they're nuts.'

From Canada comes the tale of the private pilot who was so incensed at having his flying licence revoked that he loaded a hundred pounds of pig manure into his plane, took off and 'bombed' the city of Calgary with his noisome cargo.

Further east, an Ontario newspaper reported a plane crash in the spring of 1974 when another would-be pilot, a learner this time, flew into a billboard bearing the invitation 'Learn to fly'. Oliver of Malmesbury might have had a word of advice on this.

Quite early in the space race the Zambian Minister for Space announced confidentially to the world's press that his country was planning to have a man on the moon by 1970. Not long after, reporters were invited to witness some of the high points of the astronauts' rigorous training programme. Among these they saw one unfortunate individual stuffed into a barrel, to which was fastened a rope looped round a stout tree. On a given command a team of strong assistants whirled the barrel round and round the tree. The aim, the Minister explained, was to familiarize the man with some of the problems of orbital flight.

Other phases of the training involved future astronauts being rolled downhill in oil drums and being taught to walk on their hands, claimed by the Minister to be the only way humans can walk on the moon.

As one of the crew of Apollo 8 which flew round the moon in December 1968, William A. Anders was subjected to the inevitable series of press conferences and photographic sessions after his return to earth. In a bid to escape the media and an adoring public, he took his wife to Mexico for a quiet holiday in Acapulco. Only a day or two after their arrival there was a knock at the door of their holiday villa and a young man asked if he could come inside to take some pictures. Grudgingly Anders agreed.

'Gee, thanks,' said their visitor, striding past his host to the patio. 'You've got the best view of the bay in the whole place.'

Even less impressed by the wonders of space technology was Harold Macmillan, who commented on the euphoria which greeted Yuri Gagarin when he visited London after his epoch-making space flight, 'It would have been twice as bad if they had sent the dog.'

Though with talk of manned inter-planetary travel I wonder how long it will be before announcements like that broadcast over the public address system at Heathrow a year or so ago become commonplace. 'Will Mr Seymour of Mars please go to the British Airways information desk,' asked the dispassionate voice of the tannoy.

Off the Rails

MY LOVE AFFAIR with the steam train started at a very early age. When I was about eight I began to collect train numbers. For several years thereafter I would journey on Saturday mornings to Crewe Junction where I stood with other spotters solemnly jotting down the numbers of every passing locomotive. It seems a rather curious hobby at this distance but at the time it was enormous fun. I still, however, love train travel. My wife's birthday is on New Year's Eve and it's always frightfully difficult to surprise her. Last year though I pulled off a major coup: I bought tickets on the Orient Express to Venice. It was a tremendous success and I scored several dozen Brownie points.

Departing from Victoria Station on a cold winter's day, eating a scrumptious lunch between London and Dover and then boarding the French portion of the train, which because of the festive season was decked overall with holly, mistletoe and laurel leaves, was a most agreeable way of seeing out the Old Year. Accordion players and violinists played between the hours and when we arrived in Paris a flurry of snow was already beginning to fall. Here a rather curious figure in the form of an Italian bagpipe player with a kilt that came down to his ankles got on board. We were then treated to 'Scotland the Brave' fairly endlessly until the stroke of midnight.

We went to bed. Snow was quite high between the carriages, but the sleeping car was splendidly warm. Next morning when freshly-squeezed orange juice and coffee arrived and the blinds were lifted one espied through the window a veritable fairyland. We were now in the middle of the Alps. From here, there was the gentle journey down through Italy and Venice, to be met by the red carpet and whisked away by gondola to the Danieli. It was a truly memorable journey.

This year we went off on the same train on its inaugural journey to Vienna.

The first notable railway mishap occurred not far from the lines where I pursued my boyhood enthusiasm. On 15 September 1830 the opening of the Liverpool and Manchester line was marred by the unfortunate accident which befell the Rt Hon. William Huskisson. The sixty-year-old MP who was noted for having a 'peculiar aptitude for accident', managed to get himself into the history books by becoming the first fatally injured victim of a moving train and the first railway passenger to meet his end on the rails.

According to eye-witnesses Huskisson had been travelling in the train drawn by the *Northumbrian* engine, which had come to a halt on one line, so that the Duke of Wellington and other VIPs on board might enjoy the full splendour of Stephenson's *Rocket* approaching them on the other track. Huskisson had chosen this moment to take a stroll on the line. As bad luck would have it he was spotted by the Duke of Wellington, 'between whom and Mr Huskisson some coolness had existed', by all accounts. The Duke 'made a sign of recognition and held out his hand. A hurried and friendly grasp was given, and before it was loosened, there was a general cry from the bystanders, "Get in! Get in!"' This only served to throw the doddery MP into a panic. He was still trying to get round the door into the safety of the carriage when Stephenson's train drew level and carried him off.

Immediately after the accident the victim was loaded on to the *Northumbrian* which sped off in the direction of Eccles, covering the fifteen miles in a record twenty-five minutes. Alas, even this turn of speed was to no avail. The iron horse had claimed its first victim and a bereaved public erected an eight-foot marble memorial in Pimlico to the late MP, incongruously clad in a Roman toga.

It had taken some time to convince the authorities that building the railway was a good idea in the first place. Boffins like Stephenson were in no doubt and soon became exasperated by the misgivings of laymen. One of the opponents of the scheme questioned him at a public meeting on the safety of the new transport system, 'Suppose, now, that a cow were to stray upon the line and get in the way of the engine, would not that, you think, be a very awkward circumstance?'

'Yes,' he answered tartly, 'very awkward for the cow.'

For all his absent-mindedness Isambard Kingdom Brunel (who was notorious for getting into wrong carriages and travelling long distances before realizing his mistake) shared Stephenson's fundamental understanding of railway technology. Inspecting the Birmingham railway lines on one occasion he found himself trapped between two trains rapidly steaming towards him from opposite directions. Bystanders watched with horror as he buttoned up his coat, gathered its skirts close around his legs and stood sideways on midway between the two sets of tracks. The two trains swept past leaving him a little grubbier but otherwise quite unscathed.

Another traveller with his wits about him was the chap walking along a railway line to Detroit a century ago in search of work. With his mind on other things he failed to notice the switch he trod on in which his foot became inextricably jammed. Try as he might he couldn't tug it free and the more he tugged and wrenched it, the more swollen and painful it became. He tried shouting for help, but in this isolated spot there was no one to hear. Then he heard the whistle of an approaching train – this would have thrown lesser men into complete panic. Not this resourceful fellow, however. Taking paper and linen from his bundle he made a crude torch which he fastened to the end of his stick. Then at the crucial minute he struck a match and set fire to it, allowing just enough time for the flames to catch the driver's attention before they died away.

Less fortunate was the Italian passenger who stuck his head out of his carriage window as the train pulled out of King's Cross and heard a guard yelling 'Look out' at him. He craned his head further and was rewarded a moment later by a terrible bang on the head.

'I told you to "Look out",' shouted the guard.

'But why didn't you tell me "Look in"?' screamed back the Italian, with admirable presence of mind and commendable logic.

The very existence of trains has baffled some. Dr Martin Routh, President of Magdalen, Oxford from 1791 until 1854, who died in his hundredth year and was able to count both Samuel Johnson and Cardinal Newman among his friends, resolutely refused to believe undergraduates who told him that it was possible to travel from Oxford to London in two hours on the railway line that had been opened in his eighty-ninth year. 'Conspirators bent on making me take leave of my senses,' he dismissed them.

Joining Dr Routh is the peasant from a remote region of western China who was reported enquiring about trains from one of the first outsiders to visit his home since 1949. He wanted to know if it was really true that a train was bigger than a house; that it breathed smoke and could travel hundreds of miles in a day. That was all quite true, the visitor said. But there was one final question: 'How many legs does it have?'

From India comes another tale which shows the independence of spirit with which railways have often been endowed. This concerns a traveller arriving hot and grimy at a small town in Uttar Pradesh and finding that he had to walk five miles from the station to the town centre. After struggling with his luggage for two miles he finally got a lift in a tonga. 'Why on earth did they build the station so far outside the town?' he asked the tonga driver grumpily.

'So that it would be near the railway, sahib,' the man replied.

Over the years certain railway staff have developed a masterly line in silencing difficult passengers. I like the reply given by the ticket collector to the rail traveller who arrived at Liverpool Street bright and early one morning to catch a fast train to Norwich and found it had been cancelled. He was advised to take the one that ran twenty minutes later. 'But isn't that a slow train?' he asked the man who punched his ticket at the barrier.

'Not slow,' came the reply, 'only semi-fast.'

Even if trains run on time, railway staff can't win. When British Rail instituted one of its many punctuality drives thirty years ago an unforeseen problem arose with the travelling public, many of whom began complaining that if trains ran on time they were likely to miss them. 'People have come to rely on trains being late,' explained a worried ticket collector who'd obviously had to bear the consequences of this latest management initiative. 'Now many are leaving on time and we get people dashing through the barrier at the last minute and returning to complain that they've missed their train. When we explain politely that the train left on time, they become abusive.'

British Rail's own senior management aren't immune to the risks of boarding trains at the last minute. Ten years ago, when Sir Peter Parker was BR chairman, he was on his way to a meeting with Cumbria County Council when the car carrying him to Crewe station got bogged down in traffic. Rushing to the barrier just as the train was leaving, he waved his official pass and jumped on. But as the journey got under way and familiar landmarks hove into view an uneasiness crept over him that his train was speeding away from Carlisle rather than towards it. Furthermore there was no scheduled stop before London.

As the train tore through Tamworth station, the guard tossed out a note, wrapped round a coin, in which Sir Peter had scribbled, 'Please apologize to Cumbria Council and tell them I won't be able to make it.' All he could do then was to sit back and wait for the train to reach London before he set off northwards once more – by plane.

Had Sir Peter been an ordinary member of the public he might have been treated by the guard to a reply in the tradition of that offered to a late passenger at King's Cross who jumped on to his train and asked with a sense of triumph, 'Am I all right for Finsbury Park?'

'Yes, sir,' he was told. 'Change at Peterborough.'

On the same line another guard was confronted by a woman passenger complaining that there was a very large gap under the lavatory door. Shouldn't there be some sort of warning notice, she demanded.

'What would you suggest, madam?' he asked. 'Beware of limbo dancers?'

The Nene Valley Railway operates one of those charming private lines on a stretch of railway track near Peterborough, the sort that offer a taste of old world travel by steam with all the attendant noise and dirt. One Christmas it was decided to run a 'Santa Special' and posters appeared announcing that Father Christmas would be leaving his reindeer behind and he would travel on the train, accompanied by 'elves, pixies and fairies'. Come the day of the outing, however, fairies were in rather short supply and the Santa Special chuffed off without them – to the obvious dissatisfaction of a passenger who'd taken his little son along for the ride. Later, Christmas goodwill not withstanding, he complained to the local consumer protection department that only elves and pixies were in evidence.

With passengers cast in this mould, it isn't surprising that the railway authorities are sometimes obliged to take rather extreme measures when it comes to mass communication. For instance, a BR spokesman who was asked why blank timetables had been posted at redundant stations told the *Northern Echo*, 'It is the custom in the first year after a line closes to include a timetable with no trains. It helps get the message across.'

To some regular railway travellers the actual timetables are largely works of fiction – and seemingly always have been. As far back as 1922 a report that edible snails were now being imported from France by aeroplane, was followed by the wry comment, 'It will be remembered that in the good old days when the South Eastern Railways had no rival, it was found quicker to let them walk the final stage of the journey.'

Passengers on this particular service have seldom had a completely smooth ride. In 1910 Lady Edward Cecil wrote to *The Times* complaining of 'a new experience in exaction on the part of railway officials' who had had the effrontery to weigh her ladyship's hand baggage along with her heavy luggage in the goods van. She wrote to the Managing Director of the South Eastern Railway and received a reply to the effect that all luggage, whether carried in a compartment or placed in the guard's van, was weighed, in order to ascertain the excess weight, if any.

Lady Cecil was not amused. 'This weighing of hand baggage is unique in my experience,' she wrote, 'although we who live in this part of England have learned to expect anything of the South Eastern Railway Company, which seems to devise every possible means of keeping people from travelling.'

Half a century later the decline in the service was still being lamented. 'That bowler hats appear to be falling out of favour among the supervisory grades on the railway is, in my opinion, as great a tragedy as the closing down of branch lines and other such major questions that are exercising the minds of railmen today,' wrote a correspondent to the *Daily Telegraph*.

Only a few months after the nationalization of the railways the service from Liverpool Street went through a brief period of disruption that resulted in one early evening commuter train being cancelled three nights in a row. When it was announced that their train wouldn't be running yet again, a group of businessmen, first-class season ticket holders, were heard breaking into choruses of the 'Red Flag'.

After cancelled trains, a shortage of seats comes high on the list of commuter grudges, as an irate traveller from Waterloo told the *Daily Mail* after he had got into his usual Portsmouth train and found that several compartments were locked. 'Finally a porter unlocked them,' he continued, 'inspected them – and then relocked them. "You can't go in," he announced. "There's obscene writing." Since when have British Rail appointed themselves our protectors against four-letter words? Some of us had to stand in the corridor as far as Guildford.'

It's for reasons like these that a felicitous turn of phrase in a New York travel agency's booklet about travelling in

Britain had more than a ring of truth. 'British Railways are used by all classes of the community,' it announced cheerfully. 'If you stand and watch commuters arriving at any one of the London termini you will see for yourself that they are a cross section of the population.'

The relentless drudgery of daily commuting can have quite alarming effects on the psyches of those who might otherwise seem to be perfectly level-headed people. Several years ago there was a case reported of a commuter who for no apparent reason took a swing at the genial ticket collector at his suburban station, after the railman had been passing the time of day with him for over a year. 'Evening, Bill,' the ticket collector had said in his affable way on the evening in question, to which the commuter responded with a punch on the nose. 'My name's not Bill. It's Vernon,' he later told the police.

Or there was the case of the chap who took a violent dislike to a porter at his station who was in the habit of slamming the carriage doors without regard to who or what might be caught between them and frame. So incensed did he become that he devised and executed an elaborate scheme involving a carrot and one of those gory fake thumbs that Boy Scouts use to practise their First Aid skills.

Armed with these, he stood next to a door one morning waiting for the porter to give it his customary shove. As he did so, the commuter thrust the carrot between the door and the lock, let out a piercing scream as it was crushed with a sickening crunch and dropped the dummy thumb out of the open window on to the platform. As the train pulled away he was rewarded with the sight of the guard dropping to the ground in a dead faint.

As a nation we can be remarkably selfish when it comes to putting ourselves out to make others comfortable. Let me quote the case of the traveller at Paddington who scrambled on to a crowded train bound for the West Country and found himself standing next to a compartment where the occupants had made themselves comfortable by filling vacant seats with copious amounts of luggage. For a while none of them made any move to accommodate the late arrival. Eventually someone grudgingly shifted a parcel. 'Please don't trouble yourself,' said the newcomer. 'I'm getting out at Penzance.'

As Ian Hay observed, 'An Englishman's real ambition is to get a railway compartment to himself', and passengers over the years have gone to elaborate lengths to achieve this end. Gerald Hugh Tyrwhitt-Wilson, the composer, author, painter and fourteenth Baron Berners, who built the last sizeable folly in England near his Oxfordshire home at Faringdon and kept a vintage Rolls-Royce with a clavichord mounted in the rear seat, had a foolproof method of ensuring that he travelled alone. At each station he donned dark glasses and a black skull-cap before leaning out of the window to beckon passengers inside. Few accepted the invitation. Those who had the temerity to join him didn't stay for long after he produced a large thermometer and began taking his temperature every few minutes.

Lord Halifax, at one time our ambassador to the United States, is credited with a marvellous railway ruse when he shared a compartment from Paddington to Bath with a couple of very prim ladies. The line passes through a long tunnel and when the compartment was plunged into darkness, Halifax kissed the back of his hand noisily several times. On leaving the train at Bath he rose, doffed his hat and asked, 'To which of you charming ladies am I indebted for the delightful incident in the tunnel?' and then left them to glare disgustedly at each other.

The American writer Edgar Nye had his own inventive ways of brightening long train journeys. Once, when he was travelling in the Mid-West in the company of the poet and creator of Orphan Annie, James Whitcomb Riley, he tried playing the missing ticket game with gratifying results. Nye was first to see the conductor making his way down the carriage, punching tickets, and started frantically looking for theirs with which he had been entrusted. He produced one, but searching pockets and luggage couldn't reveal the second. 'There's only one way to work this,' he hissed to Riley. 'You get down under the seat.'

So his companion clambered under the bench with considerable reluctance and lay there as the conductor approached and asked to see Nye's ticket. Nye gave him two.

'Who's the second one for?' asked the conductor.

'For my friend down there,' Nye answered.

'What's he doing down there?'

'Oh, he always travels that way,' said Nye with a smile.

The humorist James Thurber often described his mother's love of 'pranks' and he used to enjoy telling of the time when, well into her sixties, she arranged to meet an old friend at the railway station in Washington DC. The two women hadn't seen each other for thirty years and it was agreed that Mrs Thurber would be wearing a red rose in her lapel.

She arrived at the station well in advance of the train and walking around the concourse she spotted an elderly woman, a good twenty years her senior, dozing peacefully on a bench. Here was too good an opportunity to be missed and removing her rose she gently placed it in the old lady's lapel and then waited for the train to pull in.

She had no difficulty in recognizing her friend, though the latter was clearly shaken when she caught sight of the woman with the rose. Mrs Thurber watched her regain her composure before going up to the old dear, giving her shoulder a gentle shake and saying, 'Why Mame Thurber, how are you? You look just fine!'

A more serious case of mistaken identity occurred on the New York subway one morning as a young investment banker was making his way to his Wall Street office. He was standing near the doors of the train when they opened to admit passengers at one stop and a well-dressed man stepped inside, bumped into the young banker and then immediately stepped out again. He felt instinctively for his wallet and, finding it missing, grabbed at the other man, catching him by his collar. At the same time the doors closed shut, binding the banker's wrists in their rubber edges. Still he clung on, even after the train had started moving, and dragged his captive for several yards along the platform until the jacket material gave way, leaving the banker holding an inch or two of worsted. He was irritably tossing this away into the wastepaper basket in his office when his secretary buzzed to say his wife was on the telephone. She was just ringing to ask if he knew that he had left his wallet at home.

An oversight like this recalls the embarrassment of an immaculately attired City businessman who was seen being brought to Swindon station in his chauffeur-driven car one morning from his estate near Marlborough. With his chauffeur he waited for the train, still wearing his wellington boots, which he removed and handed to the chauffeur once he had taken his first-class seat. The chauffeur departed. The train pulled out. The businessman opened his briefcase and found that he had forgotten to pack his shoes inside. At Paddington he was seen shuffling towards the taxi rank with the remains of the *Financial Times* tied round his feet.

An even more bizarre chain of events led to a passenger on a Budapest-bound express spending three days in a Hungarian lunatic asylum before anyone would believe what had happened to him on the train. Admittedly this chap was an amateur bee-keeper carrying a consignment of bees in milk bottles sealed with brown paper, which demands a certain credulity from the outset.

All had gone well for the first half of the journey until the bees began to take exception to their quarters, wriggled out from under the brown paper and started wandering up the bee-keeper's legs. He explained his problem to his fellow passengers, suggesting that for their own safety and his modesty they might care to step outside while he removed his trousers and sorted out the problem. They willingly agreed. The bee-keeper opened the door and windows and gingerly removed his trousers. All of this was accomplished without mishap and he was holding them aloft wondering what to do next when a passing express train rushed by, creating a terrific airstream that whisked the trousers into the corridor and wrapped them round the head of the guard coming down the train. This was too much for the bees, and they took their revenge on the unfortunate railman. He immediately grabbed the communication cord which brought the train to a screeching halt, whereupon it promptly burst into flames.

These sudden and unexpected catastrophes proved too much for the bee-keeper, who leapt from the train in total panic and ran off in his underpants. The group of railway workers who caught him were convinced that he must have been insane and handed him over to the asylum where his story took some believing.

Sir Thomas Beecham was once travelling in a no-smoking compartment on a train belonging to the Great Western Region when he was joined by a lady who lit a cigarette as soon as she had settled herself, saying, 'I'm sure you won't object if I smoke.'

'Not in the slightest,' replied Beecham, 'provided you don't object if I'm sick.'

'I don't think you know who I am,' said his companion haughtily. 'I happen to be one of the directors' wives.'

'Madam,' Sir Thomas told her, 'if you were the director's *only* wife, I should still be sick.'

Out in the Wild West Judge Roy Bean, 'the law west of the Pecos', would have doffed his hat to Beecham for this riposte. In addition to his legal career, Bean also ran the Jersey Lily bar in the town of Langtry, Texas, close to the railway line. One hot day a train stopped to take on water and a passenger rushed in for a bottle of beer. Lazily Bean told the man to help himself. This he did, but rushed out again without paying. Livid, the good judge grabbed his gun, ran after the man, told the conductor to hold the train and found the fugitive in the smoking car, where he demanded payment for the beer. In great alarm the 'customer' handed him a ten-dollar bill. Bean pocketed this, telling the man, 'That's fifty cents for the beer, nine dollars and fifty for collecting. This squares your account. Keep the bottle.' Then he stepped down from the train and shouted to the conductor, 'You can go ahead now as soon as you damn well please.'

Fare-dodgers are a bane to railway authorities the world over. Between the wars a tea-planter in Sri Lanka arrived at

Colombo station with his wife and daughter and made the train with only seconds to spare. Having boarded without tickets, they assured the native staff on duty that they would pay at their destination. To make sure they did the duty station master wired the station to which they were travelling with the message, 'Obtain fare three Europeans travelling first-class sleeping compartment in night attire – one adult, two adultresses.'

Further north in the sub-continent the *Times of India* reported the arrest and subsequent escape of sixty fare dodgers apprehended without tickets on an express train from Lahore. They were placed under lock and key for the night at the station where they were taken from the train. In the course of their captivity there was a power cut, which plunged them into darkness. 'The ticketless ones shouted in vain,' said the spokesman of the All-India Railway Passengers Association. 'Finally they formed a pyramid of chairs and tables, gained a small roof light, and one by one stole away into the night. It was dark. Their escape went unnoticed.

'Only seven remained in the locked and darkened room,' continued the spokesman. 'They were all over eighty, some of them beggars, one insane. They could not climb the pyramid of tables and chairs. One of them, who refused to give his name, said, "What do we care? We would be happy even if we were in jail" – and that's a rather sad comment on the state of Indian railways.'

One man who happily spent the last quarter of his life living almost entirely on trains – and Italian ones at that – was Dr Francesco Saverio d'Ayla, an Italian liberal MP from the years before Mussolini's rise to power. His most valued possession turned out to be the permanent free rail pass issued to members of parliament.

While Mussolini may have set Italian trains running on time, he forced Dr d'Ayla into exile and financial ruin. When he returned after the war with barely a lira to his name, Dr d'Ayla found the railway network a convenient, if peripatetic, home. Nearing seventy when he began his nomadic existence, the former MP occasionally acquired the means to spend the night in a hotel. For the most part he travelled up and down his homeland from one railway terminus to another, chatting to other travellers (he spoke four languages), reading, sometimes sharing a snack with a generous passenger and sleeping. Mail addressed to him care of the railway police was invariably delivered within two days no matter where he happened to be. Friends and well-wishers ensured that he never went without the essentials of life, and in this way he lived out his strange odyssey, dying at the age of ninety-three with the equivalent of just one pound in his pocket.

As an actor, and one who has toured under a rich variety of conditions, I'm particularly taken with another strange tale of rail travel, this time from New Zealand and from a time when the transport system there was still in its comparative infancy. In those days touring companies lived in a continual panic between the curtain coming down on one performance and rushing to the station in time to catch the last train to their next touring date. At one town a company performing *St Joan* found that the only way they were going to catch their train was by cutting the play and they sent a cable to Shaw for permission to cut the epilogue.

In reply he cabled back, 'Permission to cut epilogue granted provided you perform it on train.'

For all the flak they receive, railways – and British ones in particular – still have a loyal and devoted following. In response to yet another tide of invective directed against our railway system a letter appeared in the *Daily Telegraph* a quarter of a century ago painting a slightly rosier picture of the national network. 'I don't think you are quite fair to British Railways or their employees,' wrote the correspondent to the editor. 'At twelve o'clock one recent Friday night I saw some happy railway porters folk-dancing at No 2 platform at Basingstoke.

'One would not have seen this before nationalization.'

I Must Go Down to the Sea Again

I THINK I can honestly claim without undue modesty that while I'm not the most accomplished of sailors, a tiny drop of our sea-faring blood still courses through my veins and makes me a moderately spirited one. I base this rather bold assertion on an experience some years ago in the South China Sea.

It actually started at a dinner party given by a friend of mine, Oliver Vaughan, in Hong Kong. He had just acquired a new ocean-going yacht and was sailing it from the boat builders in Taiwan down to his home in Singapore. After the first leg of the voyage it had been arranged that a number of friends would join him in Hong Kong for the next leg down to Manila. I was one of that happy band.

Our pre-departure dinner went very agreeably until near its close our host mentioned casually that there had been a slight change of plan. The crew that had sailed with him from Taiwan weren't in fact able to stay aboard for the whole voyage. To come more to the point, they had already flown back to Taipei. This meant that our host, and as it turned out our skipper, was now the most experienced sailor among us; and apart from a little dinghy sailing in his childhood, the sum of his experience to date amounted to the three-day cruise to Hong Kong, for a day and a half of which he had been laid low with sea-sickness.

One of our number, an eminent diplomat, magnanimously offered to vacate his place to a new crew member with greater experience and took the next flight home. The rest of us agreed to sleep on the arrangement, knowing that even if he had to sail his new boat down to Singapore alone, nothing would hold back our resourceful captain.

I felt that my own decision achieved something of an

equitable compromise. Having given my word that I would
be sailing with him, I knew that I couldn't let him down. So
I explained, 'I'm bringing a case of champagne with me and
if the going gets too rough I'm going to tie myself to the mast
and drink it.'

At this stage my appalled lawyer friend (he that smuggles
the watches) entered the lists and positively insisted that we
sought the help of the head British sailor in Hong Kong to
see whether he might be able to lend us a couple of spare
chaps for the trip. Unfortunately none were available; perhaps he didn't want to risk them with such a motley crew?
But he put us in touch with a splendid English colonel, one
Greville Egerton, MC, who together with his wife had taken
part in the South China Sea Race.

Many things went awry on the trip, particularly the snap-
ping of the mainstay. All was put right by the gallant colonel.
The only moment when we nearly sank was when I was
helming the boat into Manila harbour and we were almost
run down by a particularly large ferryboat. Other than that
our voyage passed without incident – and without undue
recourse to my emergency rations.

Ever since I've had a growing respect for all who have
answered Masefield's 'call of the running tide', even when
the odds have been severely stacked against them.

There was the case of a 51-year-old sailor who set out from
Fraserburgh on the Scottish coast bound for Great Yarmouth
in his 75-foot fishing boat optimistically named *Excelsior*.
His first landfall was at Bridlington, where he missed the
harbour entrance by 400 yards and ran aground. Undeterred,
he was refloated by the tide and negotiated the harbour at
the second attempt with only a minor collision with a jetty
and some damage to the concrete dockside.

The next leg of his voyage ended aground once again.
After being towed off he set course for Great Yarmouth and
entered the harbour unscathed. However, he was unaware
that the Haven swing-bridge, which normally opens for ship-
ping, was closed by a strike. Barely a hundred yards from
this, it dawned on our mariner that on this occasion it simply

wasn't going to open. He spun the wheel frantically and was immediately caught by the tide.

True to her name, the *Excelsior* did nothing by half measure. Her first casualty was a ketch moored alongside the wharf. Next came a dinghy. Two more craft were added to the tally on that bank, one of them a boat of some historical significance, before the *Excelsior* swung clear and the skipper tried to manoeuvre her into an empty berth on the opposite bank. It was in the course of this that she rammed a coaster. Next in line was a trimaran and only after this had been dealt a glancing blow was the *Excelsior* steered into a berth behind a 3,000-ton cargo ship. Here, as a final act of defiance, her mast became entangled in the ropes securing the ship's stern to the quay.

As he stepped ashore, bruised but unbowed, the skipper commented, 'I don't know what all the fuss is about', and then told his amazed audience that this had merely been the first leg of a voyage he was planning to Australia.

An attempt to economize on air fares persuaded an Indian living in this country to sail all the way to Calcutta. Trusting to luck and unhampered by even a modicum of sailing experience, he bought a yacht, provisioned her with several months' supply of lentils, curry powder and Quaker oats and set sail from the river Hamble. Ten miles into the voyage he ran aground and had to be rescued by the Royal Navy at a cost to the tax-payer of several thousand pounds.

More aggressive in his determination to sail away was the man spotted by holidaymakers at Margate heading towards the horizon on a pedalo. A policeman on duty set out in pursuit and was thanked for his pains by having a bottle thrown at him by the intrepid navigator as he drew alongside. 'I'm off to Amsterdam!' shouted the man as he pedalled furiously on.

At this stage the Margate lifeboat was called out, its crew augmented by five other policeman and four hours later they returned with the pedaloist clapped in irons and securely tied to a stretcher.

Then there was the spirited attempt made fifteen years ago

by a hairdresser's assistant from Kentucky to row across the Bering Straits in a bath. By way of sustenance he loaded four gallons of peanut butter into his craft, but on his fifth morning out this had gone solid. 'By late afternoon,' he went on to explain, 'although the sun was still high, the sea went rather thick. Next morning I was frozen in.' Still barely two miles from land, he abandoned his bath and walked ashore.

With the disruption to Channel crossings that seem to coincide with peak holiday periods it's interesting to reflect on the fact that three centuries ago it was possible to travel from London to France and back in the same day. William Shakespeare had been dead only three years when a chap from Andover, by the name of Bernard Calvert, proved the point on 17 July 1619. He set off from St George's Church in Southwark at three o'clock that morning and galloped south to Dover, where he arrived four hours later. There he jumped into an eight-oared barge that had been made ready for his arrival and set off for Calais. By three o'clock he had landed in France and rowed back to Dover once more, ready for the return ride to London. Thanks to careful planning, fresh horses were waiting for him along the route and shortly after eight o'clock in the evening he galloped up to St George's Church once again, in the words of a contemporary account of his feat, 'fresh and lusty'.

Over the intervening centuries the service seems to have deteriorated somewhat, leaving it to individual inspiration to speed things along. Forty years ago an army major who had been waiting six days for a passenger boat to take him from Guernsey to Jersey finally resorted to travelling in a mail steamer, wrapped up as a parcel with a label marked OHMS and accompanied by a postman.

A few years after this rumours of a serious accident on board a cross-Channel ferry circulated after a three-word telegram was transmitted by the radio officer on board the British Railways steamer *Brighton* while she was on her way to Dieppe. It read 'Just struck mine'.

By the time the ship docked at Dieppe there was a state of great alarm on both sides of the Channel and in spite of the fact that neither the ship nor any of her crew or five hundred passengers had come to any harm an official inquiry was set in motion. This revealed that the message had been one of two sent by a passenger on board the *Brighton*. A statement issued after the inquiry stated the message had been of a private nature and had been transmitted in good faith. It went on to stress that the ship was undamaged though there must have been considerable speculation as to what the passenger had been up to when he or she sent the telegram in the first place.

One thought (and not the most obvious one at that) occupied the mind of the radio operator on board the merchant ship *Tahiti*, outward bound from Sydney to San Francisco, as she slowly sank beneath the Pacific waves five hundred miles from Cook Island in one of the remotest areas of the seven seas. After sending SOS signals for sixty hours he was lifted to safety a bare quarter of an hour before the *Tahiti* went down. Even so his first question to his rescuers was, 'What's the Test match score?'

After what he'd been through you can imagine his disappointment when he discovered that he'd been picked up by an American ship and no one on board knew what he was talking about.

Doubtless a certain amount of disappointment was felt by a New Zealand yachtsman who'd shared his Pacific voyage with a cockatoo and was then charged with bird smuggling by customs officers after he had docked at home and they found the bird hidden under his bunk. In some desperation, one suspects, he tried to explain its presence, 'I was sailing from Fiji to Wellington when the bird flew into the mast and fell stunned into the cabin.'

In that case, asked the customs men, why was there also a case of bird seed under the bunk?

A reason for that was easier to conjure up. 'My wife and I like to sprinkle it on our junket,' said the yachtsman.

In the Royal Navy animals have an official capacity on board ship, at least some animals do if the 'discharge' notice that appeared in *The Times* not long after the last war is an indication. It was headed 'His Majesty's Ships Cats' and read as follows:

> Applications are invited from lovers of animals who would provide good homes for one mother and five kittens; cat is of South African parentage; kittens, born November 23, are suspected of being Javanese (either nationalist or otherwise); ship expects to arrive Chatham early January from the Far East, and delivery will be made if possible; there is no fee. Letters should be addressed to Commanding Officer, HMS *Awe*, care of Fleet Mail Office, Chatham, and marked in the left-hand top corner 'Tib-Tabs'.

As befits the Senior Service, the same attention to detail is reflected in plotting the whereabouts of ships at sea. To this end the commander of one of Her Majesty's vessels crossing the Gulf of Guinea noticed one evening that his ship, some 400 miles south of the Ghanaian coast, would be passing very close to the point where the Greenwich meridian cuts the Equator. With this in mind, he set course for it with the aim of arriving there bang on midnight. Once there, he pointed the ship's bows due north and cut the engines, thus permitting him to send the perfectly accurate signal, 'At 0000h my position Latitude 00°00' N, Longitude 00°00' E. Course 000°. Speed 0.'

Trade has always been an important side of travel and navigation especially, and for the entrepreneur trade has flourished in the least promising of conditions, like an Arctic convoy to Murmansk during the war. The Russian port is a pretty godforsaken place at the best of times, but in wartime it was even less welcoming than usual. But this didn't deter an enterprising merchant sailor from making a tidy profit from his brief stay there. He did it like this.

To begin with he left his ship with ten cigarettes in his pocket and sold them to Russians he met for a hundred roubles. He used these to buy a dozen wine-glasses and then took them on board another British merchant ship where the steward, who was in dire need of glasses, swapped them for a couple of bottles of gin.

Knowing that American ships were dry, the sailor's next call was a US cargo carrier where he exchanged the gin for 6,000 cigarettes.

Now in a really strong trading position, he went ashore once more and proceeded to sell this latest consignment for a total of 10,000 roubles. With these he bought a couple of high quality skins, sailed back home and sold them to a furrier in London for a hundred pounds!

During the war many of the great ocean liners were brought into service as troop ships, among them the mighty *Queen Mary*. Early in October 1942 she was making her way through the Irish Sea jammed full with 10,000 American troops. Escorting her on this last leg of her transatlantic voyage was the cruiser HMS *Curacao*. Her job was to protect the liner from air attack. To avoid the ever-present submarine threat the *Queen Mary* was constantly zig-zagging and since she was faster than her escort the *Curacao* had taken up a station five miles ahead. However, it was only an hour or so before the *Queen Mary* had drawn level. This coincided with another change of course on to a new zig-zag, but the liner's master assured his helmsman, 'Don't worry about the cruiser, she'll keep out of the way. These chaps are used to escorting. They won't interfere.' So the helmsman altered course and the *Queen Mary* set off on her new tack and moments later sliced the cruiser neatly in two.

The first ocean cruise undertaken solely for pleasure sailed out of New York harbour in 1867 bound for 'An excursion to the Holy Land, Egypt, the Crimea, Greece and intermediate points of interest' according to the advertisements. This was the inspiration of the celebrated Congregationalist preacher, Henry Ward Beecher, who had ideas of writing a biography of Jesus Christ and thought a trip to His homeland might be useful. This didn't explain why he felt it necessary to be accompanied by several hundred fellow travellers, though in the end he backed out of the trip and left the others to it.

The cruise cost $1,200 a head, plus a recommended $5 a

day in gold to be spent on trips ashore. Each of the passengers was put through a careful screening process to ensure that they possessed both the right social and moral credentials. Hoping to write a series of newspaper articles on the subject, Mark Twain submitted an application, but almost scuppered his chances by arriving for the interview reeking with the 'fumes of bad whisky'. However, for some unexplained reason the organizer took him for a Baptist minister and he joined the complement of otherwise worthy souls. And what a fearfully tedious lot they turned out to be.

'Three fourths of the *Quaker City*'s passengers were between forty and seventy years of age,' commented the humorist. 'The pleasure ship was a synagogue, and the pleasure trip was a funeral excursion without a corpse . . . Such was our daily life on board ship – solemnity, decorum, dinner, dominoes, devotions, slander.'

The only light relief came when Twain got ashore. As a member of the first party of American cruise passengers ever to hit Europe, he was a ready target for the eager numbers of sycophantic guides and hangers-on who stuck fast to the tourists like leeches. When the ship docked at Genoa Twain and a doctor companion were ensnared by one of these self-appointed authorities who insisted on showing them a letter in Christopher Columbus's own handwriting, which had been an enormous (and lucrative) success with every American to whom he had pointed it out. In Mark Twain and his friend he met a rather different reaction.

The two men read and looked at the letter gravely and then asked their guide exactly who this fellow Columbus was. Did he write the letter himself?

The doctor told the guide that he doubted if any self-respecting American teenager would appreciate anyone being shown a piece of his work that looked like this. Hadn't the guide any decent handwriting they could look at?

The poor guide was at his wits' end trying to explain that the letter had been written by *the* Christopher Columbus; what his handwriting looked like had nothing to do with it. To drive his point home he reminded the two Americans that Christopher Columbus had actually discovered their country.

But Mark Twain was having nothing of it. He'd just come from America, he informed the guide, and he'd heard nothing there about this Columbus fellow or any of his wild claims. Was he dead, he asked, and if so, what finished him off?

So they persisted until they finally drove away their guide distraught and more than a little perplexed, leaving them to enjoy the rest of their visit unhampered.

A rather engaging schoolboy howler defines 'wanderlust' as 'what people go on cruises for'. There are other reasons too. Some sail over the horizon just to get away for a while, like the party of a hundred passengers who boarded the good ship *World Discovery* in Norfolk, Virginia for a 'Trip to Nowhere'. Sad to say this was exactly where they ended up; they didn't even reach the horizon. Only a few miles from its berth the ship developed generator trouble and had to be towed back into port.

Others go in search of the sun, and occasionally pay a heavy price. A correspondent to the *Evening Standard* had a word or two on this subject when he wrote indignantly after one mishap to a British cruise passenger, 'If people choose to go to foreign parts in a Greek ship to avoid a British Christmas, that is their affair, and British time and money should not be spent on inquests.'

The sailing friend, to whom I made reference earlier, tells of some very bizarre 'mishaps' on cruise ships. He should know: for a long time his company was responsible for providing the nightclub entertainment on a good number of them.

One that particularly sticks in his memory was another voyage to nowhere organized by an octogenarian club in the States. This was a five-day saunter over the waves allowing the passengers to enjoy a little sea air along with all the other delights of life afloat.

In some respects – and certainly with the benefit of hindsight – it might not have been the most appropriate form of entertainment for a group of people well past their allotted three score years and ten. The sense of *joie de vivre* accompanied by substantial and frequently fairly rich meals, liberal measures of exciting drinks, not to mention the natural desire to kick over the traces, proved to be too much for several of the passengers. Not to put too fine a point on it, the first of the ship's limited supply of coffins was occupied before she had left sight of land. (As a rule Americans are not buried at sea.)

This set an unfortunate pattern for the rest of the five days. After the first few fatalities the crew allowed a degree of grim humour to leaven the situation, though the passengers never got wind of this. Indeed they found the officers more solicitous than ever. At mealtimes there were tender enquiries whenever one of the passengers failed to appear at the table. On hearing that the absentee wasn't feeling too well, further delicate questions were asked to throw light on exactly how unwell he or she might have been. Anyone watching carefully might then have noticed the officer slipping a note into the palm of a passing waiter with the whispered instruction to put the money on the best price he could get on the missing passenger. In the mounting hysteria one of the ship's company had opened a book and bets were placed among the crew on who would be the next to go. The odds lengthened and shortened dramatically as the elderly passengers failed to appear for meals or made a spirited entrance after taking a little rest.

Whatever else may be said about luxury liners, they aren't the cheapest form of entertainment; and going on a round-the-world cruise costs a pretty penny. This was certainly the reason given to the Southern Electricity Board by one of their customers for not paying her quarterly standing charge.

During that period she had been on a world cruise on the *QE2*, she explained, and as a result found herself just the tiniest bit short of cash!

Upon the Open Road

I WAS, SOME years ago, after a particularly pleasant luncheon, driving along a quiet road doing very little harm to man or beast when rounding a corner I spied ahead of me a procession. It was the day the circus left town and at the rear of the little convoy, their legs chained together, were four very large jumbos.

Unable to overtake, I pulled in behind the rear elephant's back. Or should it be in the rear of the back elephant's behind? Or even of the behind elephant's rear? Whichever it should have been, I'm sure you get the general picture.

Ahead the traffic lights turned red and we all came gently to a standstill. Now hitherto I had always thought of these particular beasts as being fairly hearty, much given to hauling logs and giving lifts to passing maharajahs. It hadn't occurred to me that sometimes they might be a trifle on the frail side. But thus it proved to be, for whilst I waited for the lights to change, the rear elephant decided to sit down. It was then that the bottom dropped into my world.

I am a little inexperienced when it comes to parking near elephants and I suppose it might be argued that it would have been wiser to have left at least two tails' lengths between the end of the procession and my bumper. With hindsight (literally) I think I would agree for the great beast sat straight on the bonnet of my car. It was as though a large grey cloud had come across the sun. Presumably the lights turned to 'go', for presently the greyness cleared as the elephant lumbered to its feet and disappeared round the corner with the rest of the procession. So intent was I on inspecting the multiple injuries to my limousine that somehow it didn't occur to me to run off in pursuit. I just contented myself with telephoning the police and then got back in the car to await their arrival.

'Nasty mess you've got there, sir,' said the sergeant, 'what happened?'

'Well, you see, officer, this elephant sat on the bonnet . . .'

'Would you mind repeating that, sir?'

'Certainly, officer,' said I. 'About half an hour ago I stopped at these lights and suddenly a great big elephant sat on my bonnet.'

'Could I trouble you to step outside the car for a moment, sir?'

I readily complied, whereupon he started to sniff at me in quite the most suspicious way. I do believe I mentioned that I had lunched especially well and it is reasonable to suppose that the aroma of the excellent burgundy lingered round my lips.

'Before you . . . er . . . saw this elephant, sir, had you by any chance consumed any beverage of an intoxicating nature?'

'Well, yes, officer, but I . . .'

He didn't let me complete the sentence but instead invited me to accompany him to his police station. Remembering the episode in the Vatican I wanted to tell him that I had been arrested in better places than where we happened at that moment to have found ourselves, but discretion seemed to be the order of the day.

Whilst they were busying themselves with their sample (which was negative of course) I asked if I might be allowed to telephone my wife. Permission was granted.

'Hello darling, the most ludicrous thing has happened, I have been arrested again.'

'Oh no!' she said, in a rather steely way.

'Yes, darling, isn't it silly! My car met with an accident and because I have had a couple of glasses of red wine they won't believe my story. Isn't it absurd?'

'What is your story?' The steel had become positively stainless.

'Well, darling, you see, this elephant sat on my car. Actually there were four of them, but only one . . .'

The phone went dead.

I don't think I will ever quite forgive my wife for hanging up on me.

Out in Africa elephants are a more common road hazard, as one would expect. In several national parks you come across signs reading 'Elephants have right of way' which may be stating the obvious but probably makes them feel good. There was absolutely no question about rights of way when a lone driver travelling through the Tanzanian bush came upon a large bull elephant standing four square in the middle of the road. In the drama of the moment the driver panicked somewhat, crunched to a halt and dived underneath his Land-Rover for cover. The elephant obviously thought this was rather amusing and wandered round the car to have a closer look. He nudged the back and found that it moved. So he nudged it again. In his haste the driver had forgotten to put on the handbrake.

With nothing better to do that afternoon, the elephant decided to nudge his new toy a bit more and started pushing the Land-Rover along the dirt track. Underneath the driver had no option but to wriggle along with it. And so he wriggled for nearly three quarters of a mile until the Land-Rover ran off the track and got stuck in a hollow. At this point the elephant got a bit bored with it and sauntered off into the bush, leaving the motorist with extremely raw elbows and a pair of trousers he wouldn't be able to wear in company again.

You wouldn't expect elephants to pose much of a road hazard in this country; at least I certainly didn't and nor I suspect did the chap who took his family to a wildlife park and had one of the doors kicked in by an elephant in a bad mood. The driver, as you might imagine, was a bit shaken up by this and without stopping to remonstrate with the petulant pachyderm took off to find a stiff drink – well, several, if the truth be told.

He drove home very carefully, mind you, and was able to pull up perfectly safely when a minor pile-up happened a few cars ahead.

The police arrived and began asking the motorists whether

or not they had been involved. Quite truthfully the driver denied that he had had anything to do with the minor contretemps up ahead.

'Would you mind explaining how this happened, then, sir?' asked one of the policemen, indicating the crumpled car door.

'An elephant kicked it in, officer,' he said ingenuously.

'Did it really, sir? Perhaps you'd better breathe into this bag for me.'

The driver puffed away with resignation and the little crystals told their damning tale.

One chap who got off a bit more lightly was the Rolls-Royce owner spotted spending a penny beside the M1 very late one evening by policemen in a patrol car. One of the policemen asked him what he thought he was up to, to which he replied that he thought it was pretty obvious. Having been caught short between service areas, he had taken a chance and pulled up to relieve himself on the verge.

Had he been drinking, he was asked.

He said he had, and out came the breathalyser which gave an uncompromisingly positive reading.

One of the officers took the incriminating little bag off to the station while the other said he would follow along behind driving the Rolls and its owner. Only after his colleague had sped off and he had walked up to the driver's door did he see the chauffeur who had been waiting patiently for his boss to finish his pee before continuing their journey!

Although the majority of the drivers in the States observe the fifty-five mile an hour speed limit, and consequently drive far slower than most of us, officers of the Highway Patrol in Indiana were taken by surprise when they came across a motorist moving at walking pace down the centre of an eight-lane interstate highway. Having escorted the driver over to the hard shoulder to find out what he was doing they were told, 'I was looking for my dentures, which got thrown out of the window by accident when they got stuck in the wing of a chicken leg I was chewing.'

Speeding is a more common misdemeanour around the

world for which a variety of inventive replies have been offered over the years. An Israeli policeman who pulled over a motorist whizzing past him thought there was something vaguely familiar about the eye-patch he was wearing and realized why when he walked up to the driver's door and saw the Defence Minister, Moshe Dayan, looking up at him and asking what the matter was.

The policeman explained that he had been driving too fast.

'I've only got one eye,' Dayan told him. 'What do you want me to watch – the speedometer or the road?'

There was a Wiltshire driver who ended up in front of the magistrates after being overtaken by a police patrol and made to stop for speeding. He told the bench that he'd been reading a copy of the Highway Code at the time.

But perhaps the most striking deterrent was devised by a road safety committee in Pennsylvania. They put up a traffic sign reading, 'Caution – nudists crossing'.

Today it's easy to look back fondly to the early days of motor travel, to a time when the open road lay clear and unobstructed before you, when there were few other motor vehicles to hinder your passage and fewer policeman to spoil your fun. In reality, it was never quite that straightforward. In 1895, for example, there were only two cars in the entire state of Ohio, with an area not appreciably smaller than that of England. Nevertheless they still managed to run into each other.

Up in the Highlands of Scotland many years ago, a spirited young driver in an open-topped tourer was enjoying himself enormously speeding along a winding mountain road. No vehicle had passed him for miles and with a burst of youthful indiscretion he tackled the next hairpin bend on the wrong side of the road. That day Dame Fortune wore an indulgent smile, for as he came round the bend he saw another car approaching driven by an equally exhilarated but momen-tarily petrified driver who had also decided to take the bend on the wrong side. So it was that both cars passed. Safely round the bend they stopped. Their drivers got out pale and unspeaking, shook hands without a word and drove off rather more sedately.

From more recent times comes the story from West Germany of a couple of men driving along one very foggy winter morning. So poor was the visibility that they were both forced to crane their heads out of their windows to follow the white line down the middle of the road. And so intent were they on following this that they each failed to see the other approaching. Their heads met with an awful bang and put them both in hospital.

An even more improbable prang happened in the Czech capital, Prague, when an elderly pedestrian started to cross a busy street when the pedestrian warning light was showing red. The driver of an oncoming car saw him just in the nick of time and slammed on his brakes. This threw his car into a skid during which one of the back doors opened and a girl travelling in the back seat was thrown out. The car came to a halt by the kerb and another pedestrian who had seen the near miss rushed over to it and found the driver dazed but unhurt and an elderly woman crying beside him. But as it turned out this was very much a family affair.

The police called to the scene of the accident discovered that the elderly man who had crossed the road was the father of both the driver who'd missed him and the girl who had fallen into the road. And just to complete the homely picture the old woman crying in the car was his wife. Even more amazing is that none of them was hurt.

Driving through Hollywood one day in a carefree daze Beatrice Lillie allowed her car to stray on to the left-hand lane and only regained her composure when an imminent head-on collision obliged her to swerve violently off the road. Her car was a write-off but she staggered out with merely a few cuts and bruises and stumbled to the nearest house. The door opened to reveal the film star John Gilbert who asked in astonishment what she was doing there.

'Heard there was a party,' gasped Bea. 'Came.'

Down in Texas nemesis struck a lady driver in Houston whose car bore the bumper sticker 'Don't follow me, I'm lost'. This proved to be as good as its word when she mistook the open doors of a roll-on-roll-off ferry for a garage exit and careered through into the murky waters beyond.

Invariably there's something a trifle smug and condescending in the manner of the rescue firms that arrive to extricate one from predicaments like this and it's gratifying to discover that just once in a while they too end up with egg on their faces. One such case came to light in San Diego, where a motorist got his car well and truly stuck in the mud of San Diego bay. He called in a highway rescue firm. They arrived with a tow-lorry and proceeded to get this stuck too. Their back-up tow-lorry was called and met the same fate. Realizing that something rather special was now called for, the proprietor hired an amphibious rescue craft. But that also got bogged down. In desperation by now, he had no choice but to obtain the services of a massive bulldozer which eventually succeeded in dragging out all four stranded vehicles. This little exercise cost the highway rescue firm an estimated $16,000. The driver of the original car got off scot free!

Across the Pacific, twenty-eight members of a New Zealand weight-watchers' club paid a more humiliating price when they climbed back on to their bus during an outing one hot summer day and the wheels promptly sank up to their axles in the tarmac of the car park!

Inevitably it's the insurance companies who have to sort out these unfortunate mishaps, a job which isn't made any easier by some of the accident reports they receive from their clients. 'Coming home I drove into the wrong house and collided with a tree that I don't have,' wrote one contrite driver to his insurers.

'I collided with a stationary bus that was coming the other way,' explained another.

'One wheel went into the ditch, my feet jumped from the brake to the accelerator, leapt across the other side of the road, and jumped into the trunk of a tree,' wrote a third.

When it comes to running over people, the motoring public can be more brazen still. 'The other man altered his mind, so I had to run over him,' was one driver's account of the glancing blow he dealt a passer-by. 'A pedestrian hit me and went under the car,' was the novel reasoning adopted by a chap who found himself in the same predicament.

The line of argument that has always appealed to me when it comes to motor travel was that taken by a coroner who responded to evidence that foreigners drove on the right in their own countries with the comment, 'It seems to me a shame that they cannot make regulations on the Continent identical to those in this country.' He might have appreciated the attention to detail adopted by a learner driver who took the wheel for her first driving lesson and attached a piece of paper to it reading, 'Left is the side my wedding ring is on.'

Clearly a similar, though diametrically opposed, anxiety plagued the lady member of the RAC who wrote to their route planning department requesting directions from Birmingham to Bristol that would allow her to make the journey without the need to turn right! After a little head-scratching they were able to oblige, though she ended up driving over twice the distance of the more orthodox and dare one say ambidextrous route.

Twenty years ago, when London traffic was starting to boom (literally) planners in the Westminster City Council highways department came up with a splendid scheme for keeping Pimlico relatively free of traffic. Their idea centred on the creation of a motoring maze that would get through drivers so completely perplexed by the time they found their way out that they would be warned off ever entering the area again. (Some might argue that the scheme has been very successfully adopted in various parts of the metropolis.)

Travelling by car in other countries introduces a fresh range of hazards. Motorists in Tanzania apparently pass a sign at a petrol station on the edge of the Serengeti Plain that warns, 'Last chance for fuel. Next three stations are mirages.'

In Naples a lady driver put her arm out of the window to make a hand signal – allowing a quick-witted mugger to remove £500 worth of jewellery from her wrist.

Many people take their cars with them on Continental holidays, and in some respects only compound their travelling problems. In one celebrated case a couple taking their caravan as well cut it very fine when driving back to the Channel, so fine in fact that the husband had to drive non-stop through the night to arrive at Calais in time for the crossing. His wife decided she might as well take advantage of the comfort of the caravan and snuggled down inside as he raced across northern France. At one point her husband pulled into a lay-by to spend a penny. Taking advantage of the stop, his wife nipped out to do the same. But the driver finished before his passenger and having no idea that she had left the caravan, he got back behind the steering-wheel and drove off.

Luckily for her, the next car to pass was another English one also heading for the Channel ports; and since this wasn't towing a caravan it was able to catch up with her husband. Nevertheless it took the lady a fair amount of explaining to account for hanging around a lay-by at two in the morning covered in nothing but a see-through nightie and considerable confusion.

A young Californian man mislaid his wife on the day they were married after their car had got stuck in sand near the town of Holtville. After trying to shift it without success, he left car and bride and set out to find a breakdown lorry. When he returned with help a couple of hours later neither of them was anywhere to be seen.

The newlyweds ran into each other by chance the next day as he was driving through another town, slightly bewildered. Reunited with him, his bride calmly explained that a stranger had managed to free the car after he had left and had taken her to Mexicali across the Mexican border, so that they could both 'let their hair down'.

Travelling by taxi can have its exciting side too, especially when it offers a touch of the unexpected. One day an Athenian taxi driver picked up a man who'd flagged him down and was a bit taken aback when his fare gave his very own address and asked to be taken there. So he dropped the man outside his front door, took his money and watched with mounting surprise as the other chap calmly produced a key and let himself in. A moment or two later the taxi driver let himself in with his own key and discovered his passenger and his wife *in flagrante delicto*.

'It wasn't his lucky day,' commented the driver with remarkable equanimity. 'Athens has 70,000 taxis.'

The American revue and television star Carol Burnett climbed out of a taxi one day and accidentally shut her coat in the door. Neither she nor the driver realized this until he had started to move away and to avoid being pulled off her feet, the comedienne had no option but to run alongside. Luckily someone on the pavement saw what had happened and yelled at the driver to tell him. He stopped instantly and after releasing Miss Burnett's coat asked, 'Are you all right?'

'Sure,' she answered, panting for breath, 'but how much more do I owe you?'

There are even those who can find excitement in taxi numbers. As he was lying in a London hospital near the end of his life the Indian mathematician Srinivasa Ramanujan was visited by his old friend the celebrated Cambridge mathematician G. H. Hardy. Hardy went to see him regularly and seldom saw signs of improvement. On this occasion he was particularly downcast by his friend's condition and, desperate for something to say, told him, 'The number of my taxi was 1729. It seemed rather dull.'

'No, no, Hardy!' Ramanujan replied. 'It is a very interesting number. It is the smallest number expressible as the sum of two cubes in two different ways.'

I only wish when I travel by taxi the meter would show the smallest number expressible in any way.

Entente Cordiale

IN SPITE OF the best endeavours of Edward VII to harmonize Anglo-French relations, history and an inherent suspicion on both sides of the Channel have left an indelible dividing line setting the two nations apart.

Half a century ago a letter appeared in the *Cambridge Times* indicative of the distrust felt by many of our fellow countrymen for all things foreign and offering an engagingly simple safeguard against them. 'Those of us who know the Continental Sunday,' it read, 'have no wish to see it introduced here. It is the cause of all the trouble on the Continent.'

More recently I heard of an English couple staying at a hotel in Devon who were offered a choice at breakfast. 'Would you like the full English breakfast or the Continental?' asked the waiter.

'Oh, we don't want any of that foreign muck,' said the wife. 'Just bring us some rolls and coffee.'

Offering a full English breakfast is one of the few times when you can actually discomfit a Frenchman. There's nothing more satisfying than for one's French guests, who have come downstairs in the morning cheerfully anticipating their *petit déjeuner*, to discover on the hotplate kedgeree, devilled kidneys, bacon, eggs, mushrooms, sausages and perhaps the occasional kipper, together of course with porridge. It is the last-mentioned that causes the greatest distress. Firstly they can't identify it, and then they are not sure of the batting order. If left alone they generally decide it's a rather curious English pudding and attempt to consume it out of sheer politeness at the end of the meal.

Twenty-five years ago a Midlands family crossed the Channel for a fortnight and recorded an unusual triumph in the *Leicester Mercury* when they got home. 'We went to

France for our holidays and took six sliced loaves of bread with us,' they informed their fellow readers. 'We still had one left after thirteen days. It was still good to eat. This is a tribute to a Leicester bakery' – it's also another reason for the French to look on our gastronomic priorities with a sense of complete bewilderment.

A few years earlier a cry of outrage was raised in the *Recorder* when a reader wrote to say, 'I was horrified in a recent broadcast about winemaking in France that the maker, a large man with rolls of fat, stripped and got naked into the vat to stamp on the must . . .No more French wines for me until they bathe in the normal manner.'

And it was the issue of bathing that so incensed a man from Bradford that he wrote to his local paper following his first holiday abroad, a week in Dieppe, complaining that the French were a wilful race and it was little wonder that the Common Market was getting itself into such a mess. 'What can you do,' he asked rhetorically, 'with a nation who arrange all their plumbing so that hot water always runs out of the tap marked "C"? I found this to be the case wherever I tried to wash my hands and in spite of numerous complaints no action was ever taken.'

Mind you, we can be pretty perverse about making others feel at home when we put our minds to it. In an effort to discourage the unwanted attention of French schoolchildren on holiday in Britain a shopkeeper posted notices reading, 'La direction regrette de se voir obligée de refuser l'entrée de cet établissement aux Étudiants Français.' Asked who had devised these for him, the proprietor replied, 'It was done by a lady connected with the "Come to Britain" movement. She knew French.'

That was about all, it would seem.

The Irish author, Brendan Behan, was given the opposite commision by a café proprietor in Paris who wanted to attract English tourists. Behan had been a housepainter by trade and undertook to paint one of the café windows. His message of welcome went like this:

Come in, you Anglo-Saxon swine
And drink of my Algerian wine.
'Twill turn your eyeballs black and blue,
And damn well good enough for you.

He pocketed his money and beat a hasty retreat before the café owner had the window translated.

On the whole, efforts to improve relations between the two nations have had a more positive response in the last fifty years. As an optimistic correspondent to *The Bicycle* remarked in the early 1950s, 'The British cyclist making friends with all kinds of foreigners all over Europe is helping to ensure that Shropshire and Suffolk will still be on the map in twenty or thirty years.' (We nearly lost Shropshire when they tried to call it Salop several years ago, but for once the blame for that couldn't be laid at the door of the EEC or our French neighbours.)

At about the same time the manners of English men came in for praise from a French visitor who was moved to write to the *Sunday Dispatch*, 'I am a French girl staying in London for the language, and am surprised by the politeness of your English men, but only over the age of about fifty, who remove their hats in lifts and buses and lower their eyes.'

Perhaps an even greater sensitivity was displayed by French officials during a visit once made to Corsica by the Queen and the Duke of Edinburgh. After searching the island for a car they considered 'splendid enough' for their royal visitors (it was still a time when the island was considerably less well off than the mainland of France), the Corsicans in charge of the arrangements were forced to think again when they discovered that the car's owner had been divorced. It was felt that this might have embarrassed Her Majesty.

In more recent years even ordinary visitors to France have met with greater sympathy than popular perception might lead one to believe. In 1981 an English couple, Mr and Mrs Thomas Eltham, treated themselves to a day trip to Boulogne. There they shopped and saw the sights and enjoyed just wandering about in a foreign town. In fact they enjoyed themselves so much that they strayed rather further from the centre than they had intended and since neither could speak or read a word of French the consequences were a bit alarming. They spent a good part of the afternoon walking around the outskirts of Boulogne. Several people kindly offered them lifts, but these only helped to confound their predicament and night had fallen when they finally arrived at the railway station.

The return ferry had long since left and in a move of some desperation they bought tickets from Boulogne to Paris which used up most of their money. 'But when we got off at the station,' said Mrs Eltham, taking up the story, 'we found that we were in Luxembourg and not, as we had thought, in Paris. Furthermore, it was by now Tuesday morning and not as we had hoped only Monday night.'

Fortunately the police in Luxembourg proved to be kindness itself and put the now exhausted couple on the first train bound for the French capital.

Relieved that their troubles seemed to be over at last they both fell asleep and slept so soundly that when they came to they discovered that they'd somehow missed Paris altogether and furthermore travelled right through France to Basle.

'The Swiss police sent us back to France,' continued Mrs Eltham, 'and the French police at Belfort on the frontier said we should go to Montbeliard and there catch the Boulogne connection.'

With only a few francs between them, they decided to walk the twenty-four kilometres to Montbeliard where the town council generously put them up in a hostel free of charge. They desperately needed money for the journey home and tried to find a couple of jobs that would earn them the return fare. After a week of fruitless searches which weren't aided by the language barrier or the fact that unemployment was already distressingly high in the area, the local police put them on a train back to Belfort – and square one, so to speak.

'It was dark when we reached Belfort,' explained Mrs Eltham, 'and somehow or other we lost our way. In the end

Greetings in Singapore

From Kashmir to Kensington.
I bought the wolf-skin outfit
from a chap in Srinagar
(*Sunday People/Keystone*)

The front at St Maxime during the year we spent in the South of France   (*Ron Keightley*)

Early days under sail *en famille*

Harpooned in Fiji

The King and I. (Meeting His Majesty the Yang Dipertuan Agung
in Kuala Lumpur before I changed his seating arrangements)

On the footplate of a 'Black Five'   (*Albert Clarke*)

A day at the races   (*Maidenhead Advertiser*)

we decided to walk the sixty-two kilometres to Vesoul. Then our luck changed. A lorry driver gave us a lift.'

A few days later, travel-weary but relieved, they were in Paris and waiting for a Channel-bound train at the Gare du Nord. However, France hadn't quite let go her grip on the Elthams. Instead of a train to Boulogne they managed to get on to one heading for Bonn!

The West German police didn't beat about the bush and sent them straight back to the frontier.

'This time things turned out for the best,' the Elthams said. 'A French policeman actually drove us to Boulogne where we spent twenty-four hours with the customs authorities.'

After this they managed to land on home soil without further mishap where the passport authorities turned a blind eye to their slightly extended 'day trip', leaving the Elthams to walk the last twenty-odd miles back home.

Restored to the comfort and tranquillity of familiar surroundings the gallant duo reviewed their extended Continental tour in the light of earlier trips to distant parts. 'The previous year we had gone to the Isle of Wight,' explained Mr Eltham. 'We shall not be going abroad in future.'

At the very end of the Napoleonic Wars one traveller turned up in the unexpected surroundings of the battlefield at Waterloo. It was the Duke of Wellington who first spotted him, riding about in the thick of the fire in civilian clothes. He beckoned him over to ask what he was doing and found that he was an Englishman who happened to be in Brussels and, never having seen a battle, thought he would take a look at this titanic struggle. The duke pointed out that he was in imminent danger of losing his life, to which he replied, 'Not more than your grace,' and rode off.

Over the next hour or so, Wellington caught sight of the chap riding about among the cannon shot and smoke. At one time when he needed a messenger and none was available he hailed him again and asked him to take an order to charge to a regiment stationed a little way off. Carrying some mark of authority that the colonel would recognize, the messenger galloped off and minutes later Wellington saw his order obeyed. When the little man galloped back, Wellington asked him for his card, which he finally looked at later that evening after the victory had been secured.

His messenger, it transpired, was a button manufacturer from Birmingham, and when he was next in the city he enquired after the firm and discovered that the man who had ordered the charge was indeed their travelling salesman.

For a year and a half we lived in the south of France and for all the time we were in our small village I struggled away in my terrible French trying to communicate with our neighbours. It was only when we were finally leaving and we threw a little party to say goodbye to all our now dear *amis*, that I discovered that most of the people with whom I had been having such desperate conversations over the eighteen months could actually speak totally fluent English. Not a word of this had been revealed during the whole time we spent there.

With language lying at the root of so many little Anglo-French misunderstandings, one can understand, if not condone, the furious tirade of an English traveller at the Gare de Lyon berating an unfortunate porter with the inspired outburst, 'Je vous avoir savoir que je ne suis pas quelqu'un que vous trifler avec.'

The artist James Whistler was staying in Paris once when he came across an Englishman in a restaurant experiencing some difficulty making his order intelligible to the waiter. Whistler offered his help, only to be rebuffed by the man replying stiffly that he could make do quite well on his own.

'I fancied the contrary just now,' Whistler replied, 'when I heard you desire the waiter bring you a pair of stairs.'

A fellow Englishman with a marginally better grasp of the language settled himself at a café table in Paris for lunch and ordered soup to begin with. When the waiter brought it, he noticed a fly swimming on the surface and drew his attention to it, 'Regardez – un mouche.'

The waiter shook his head. 'Non, monsieur,' he replied. 'C'est *une* mouche. Féminine, n'est ce pas?'

'My word,' exclaimed the diner, 'you've got damned good eyesight.'

On the subject of soup, an Englishman booked to stay in a hotel in Annecy for a week picked up the lunch menu on the third day and saw that 'Soupe de jour' was listed at its head as usual and exclaimed to his wife, 'What, again?'

And English visitors were far from willing to accept the generous offer made by a café proprietor in Brittany whose tables bore the message, 'Carafe d'eau du patron gratuite'.

In an effort to establish a civil relationship, two guests staying at a hotel in Biarritz, one English, the other French, began to exchange formal greetings in the dining-room. Neither spoke the other's language so when the Frenchman wished his neighbour 'Bon appétit', the Englishman misunderstood and thought he was announcing his name.

'Robinson,' he said in reply.

This pleasant exchange took place over the next few days until the Englishman happened to mention Monsieur Bon Appétit to a French-speaking friend, who pointed out that this wasn't the man's name; he was merely wishing him a pleasant meal.

At the next opportunity the Englishman was the first to speak, saying 'Bon appétit' with a smile.

Gravely the Frenchman nodded his head and answered, 'Robinson.'

On the occasion of General de Gaulle's retirement as President of the Fifth Republic in 1969 he and Madame de Gaulle were lunching with English friends when the conversation turned to what they would both be doing in the years ahead. The former first lady was asked what she was most looking forward to and replied without hesitation, 'A penis.'

Conversation round the table faltered momentarily until the General gently corrected her inflection. 'My dear, I think the English don't pronounce the word quite like that. It's "'appiness".'

On her first visit to Paris the American comedy character actress Marie Dressler, known the world over to be a fine figure of a woman, stayed at the Hotel Continental. One day she exhausted her very sketchy French trying to obtain directions from a taxi driver. The address she wanted was only just behind the hotel, as he kept repeating, 'C'est derrière l'hôtel, madame.'

In the end she gave up and asked him, 'Que signifie le mot "derrière"?'

Shrugging his shoulders the taxi driver replied, 'If madame does not know the meaning of "derrière", nobody does!'

For all our national reticence the Académie Française must surely take some pleasure in the growing awareness and use of French on this side of the Channel. Workmen repainting Westminster Bridge had the courtesy to put up a notice warning passers-by, including foreign tourists, 'Le paint est wet.'

Then there are all those menus and mouth-watering dishes that always sound much more inviting when offered in the language of truly *haute cuisine* – dishes like 'Kipper sur toast' presented by a Lyons Corner House from the days when they still existed, or the equally inviting 'Steak Pie du Cottage' that once graced a luncheon menu at the Savoy.

On the other hand the Académie might have been a little less enthusiastic about another import of sorts which was boldly advertised in the *Ashby Times* thirty years ago:

FOLIES PARISIENNE

See! Nudes in the Waterfall
Daring fan dance. Virgin and the Devil
Sensational Dance of the Strip Apache
Les Beaux Mannequins de Parisienne
Continental and Oriental Nudes

Old Age Pensioners – Monday

I suspect they would have preferred that particular measure of our *entente cordiale* to have been a little more diluted.

On a personal note, my wife and I have always had

a tremendous affection for France and for the Riviera in particular. We spent our honeymoon in Juan Les Pins and it was there, on the second night of our marriage, that I discovered at two in the morning that my poor wife suffered from asthma (an affliction which has now thankfully passed). Her breathing was coming more and more fitfully and I became deeply alarmed as she was standing at the bedroom window gasping for breath. Being the middle of the night I wasn't quite sure how to get help, so I went along to the Carlton in Cannes and asked if they could provide me with an English-speaking doctor.

This they were able to do and within half an hour he arrived. Now, the French treat pretty nearly everything from rheumatism and certainly a headache with a suppository. This was duly prescribed for my wife and the doctor said, 'Madame, would you please take this and insert it in your anus?'

The suppository disappeared beneath the sheets and there wasn't a movement. The doctor asked tentatively, 'Madame, you have put it in your anus?'

My wife nodded demurely, replying, 'Oh yes.'

'Are you absolutely sure?'

'Yes, doctor.'

At which point he shrugged his shoulders and departed.

Now, Latin has never been my wife's strong suit and it was only after the doctor had left the room that we discovered she had put it in the wrong place.

We have been married for well over thirty years now and each year we still revisit the small pension where we spent that enormously romantic honeymoon all those years ago – she goes in June and I go in August.

English as a Foreign Language

I'M SURE THAT it must strike other nations as more than a touch ironic that the British traveller, who surely ranks among the world's worst at mastering foreign languages, should take such undisguised pleasure in the minor solecisms of others battling with our absurdly irregular tongue.

It has to be admitted that a good many of these slips do afford a modicum of gentle amusement, while others lend a richness and originality few native speakers could rise to.

For over a century now one particular publication has set a standard in this respect that few have equalled. I refer of course to the notable work of Pedro Carolino, compiler of that indispensable phrasebook *The New Guide of the Conversation in Portuguese and English* now popularly known as *English As She Is Spoke*.

As he modestly states in the preface, Senhor Carolino devised this little classic as 'A choice of familiar dialogues, clean of gallicisms, and despoiled phrases, it was missing yet to studious portuguese and brazilian Youth; and also to persons of other nations, that wish to know the portuguese language . . .'

To aid him in this worthy pursuit he made extensive use of his command of French, or rather his Portuguese–French dictionary, which calls into question his comment on 'gallicisms' above. Indeed this inconsistency was further compounded by the fact that he arrived at his chosen English phrases via this dictionary and a French–English one. The vital volume missing from his library was a Portuguese–English dictionary. Though had he possessed one, what a gem the world of scholarship would have lost.

Under one of his 'Dialogos Familiares', 'The French Language', the author hints at the debt he owed to this novel approach to international communication:

'Do you study?'
'Yes, sir, I attempts to translate of french by portuguese.'
'Then you learn the french language? You do well the french language becomes us all days too much necessary. What books have you there?'
'It is a grammar and a vocabulary.'
'Do you know already the principal grammars rules?'
'I am appleed my self at to learn its by heart.'
'It is a collection choice pieces in prose.'

Choice indeed.
Senhor Carolino had a pretty disparaging view of the world of books in general. Here he is talking 'With a bookseller':

'What is there in new's literature?
'Little or almost nothing, it not appears any thing of note.'
'And yet one imprint many deal.'
'That is true; but what is imprinted. Some news papers, pamphlets, and others ephemeral pieces: here is.'

Not that his view of mankind was much rosier. Getting on with people can't have been helped by conversation peppered with 'Familiar Phrases' like:

Speak me more frankly.
He has spit in my coat.
We are all mortal.
He laughs at my nose, he jest by me.
I have a mind to vomit.
He caresses all women.
One's find modest and young man rarely.

Turning to 'Idiotisms and Proverbs' his rather earnest approach to life is reflected in his choice of well-known sayings like:

He has the throat paved.
He steep as a marmot.
To build castles in Espagnish.
The stone as roll not heap up not foam.
A take is better than two you shall have.
To eat of the cow mad.
The dress don't make the monk.
He sin in troubled water.
Of the hand to mouth, one lose often the soup.

not to mention the stark foreboding of 'Belly famished has no ears.'

At least his table offered imagination and variety. Under 'Fishes and Shellfishes' he lists: bleak, shad, whale, barbel, calamary, conger, dolphin, dorado, a sort-e of fish, hedgehog, snail, wolf, muscles and torpedo.

Favourite dishes come under the heading 'Eatings' and include mouth-watering delights like: a sirloin of beef, some fritters, a stewed fruit, some sugar plum, some wigs, a chitterling sausages and a dainty dishes.

Had you been taken ill under Senhor Carolino's roof he would have been able to diagnose any one of a number of ailments: the apoplexy, the scrofulas, the bloody-flux, the fluxion, the itch, the gout, the jaundice, the melancholy, the megraine, the vomitory.

Remedies were close at hand too: the cataplasm, the cautery, the decoction, the gargarism, the marsh-mallow, the laudanum, the bleeding and the vomitory [again].

But it was as a lover that his command of English reached its poetic heights. 'My handsome angel,' he addressed the fictional object of his passion:

You are divined.
That may dead if I lie you.

I don't love too much ceremonies.
What murmure you?
You make grins.
I know there are a thousand insurmoutable difficulties.
Have you understanded?
Undress you too.
Tell me that you like more.
No budge you there.
Why you push me?
We are all mortal.

One can't help admitting that a phrasebook cast in this mould brings a refreshing vitality to a genre dominated in more recent times by the robust cheerfulness of the Berlitz school. As Pedro Carolino himself would have been the first to admit, 'A bad arrangement is better than a process.' And who are we to argue?

Touching on Senhor Carolino's 'thousand insurmountable difficulties' I am reminded of the radio correspondent who had the honesty to admit many years ago, 'My knowledge of foreign languages is rather shaky, and they always seem harder to understand on the air except when an Englishman is speaking them.'

Set against this is the experience of one of that rare breed of English-speakers who is a master of languages. This particular fellow, an American academic as it happens, had adopted Italy as his second home, in the course of which he had acquired several national characteristics, one of which was an engagingly cavalier approach to authority. Travelling once with a companion he decided to visit Venice and having boarded the train in Rome looked along the corridors for a couple of suitable seats. The train was crowded and the only seats offering a degree of privacy and comfort were both marked 'reserved'. Nevertheless, our man settled himself into one of these and told his companion to do the same.

'But they're reserved,' said his friend.

'Never mind. This is Italy,' came the reply.

Only a couple of minutes after the train had pulled away

from the platform, a Dutch couple, laden with luggage and perspiring heavily, struggled into the compartment bearing tickets that clearly showed them to be the owners of two reserved seats. Politely they tried to acquire these, but the American studiously refused any sign of comprehension.

This obviously annoyed the Dutch husband, who stalked off and returned a couple of minutes later with the guard, brandishing his tickets. In a rattle of Italian the guard asked what the problem was. The Dutchman struggled with a few incoherent words that only served to exasperate the guard, who turned to the American.

Now he broke his silence in a cascade of eloquent Italian that would have had Beatrice swooning at this feet. The guard was clearly jolly impressed as well, for he smiled broadly, said something else and then bustled the Dutch couple, still waving their tickets, out of the door and closed it.

'We owe these seats to a rare use of the Italian subjunctive,' said the professor to his friend. 'Don't waste time asking questions – I'll explain everything in the bar.'

There's a great deal to be said in favour of mugging up even a few elementary phrases before setting foot on foreign soil, as a visitor to Naples discovered when she realized she was the only member of a tour party able to read the sign posted on a staircase in one of the city's monuments. 'This staircase is in a dangerous condition', it read. 'It will be closed at the end of the tourist season.'

One of the few phrases that I know in Cantonese is 'qong qi fat choi' (?) which roughly means 'Happy New Year'. This, as you can imagine, has a tolerably limited use. However, it came into its own in the unlikely setting of the Orient Express, on the occasion of the surprise birthday treat for my wife to which I have already alluded. On our way into the dining-car for dinner, I noticed a young Chinese couple sitting at the upper end of the carriage. As midnight approached, the musicians struck up 'Auld Lang Syne', the last moments of the Old Year were proclaimed and with champagne corks popping and streamers being thrown, everyone started wishing each other a happy New Year. This was my big opportunity. I rushed round to the other end of the carriage and found the young Chinese couple still sitting there. 'Qong qi fat choi,' I said.

They looked at me blankly.

'Qong qi fat choi,' I repeated slightly more slowly, worried about my pronunciation.

There was still no response.

'Qong qi fat choi,' I said quite loudly and very deliberately.

Solemnly they produced their railway tickets from their pockets and handed them to me. It turned out that they were Japanese and thought I was the ticket inspector. Ah well . . .

Among the refugees to flee Hungary after the revolution thirty years ago was a man who had been something of a celebrated oarsman during his youth. He duly found his way to this country and was soon taken up by the rowing fraternity beside the River Thames, from whom he acquired most of his rudimentary English. The senior figures in the rowing world took a kindly interest in him too and he was often invited to rather grand gatherings by these kindly old men. At one very posh do he enjoyed himself enormously and it was with genuine regret that he sought his hostess at the end of the evening to make his departure.

'Thank you for a very nice evening,' he said, shaking her hand, 'but now it is time I bugger off.'

Official interpreters are usually so accomplished in their task of communicating between heads of state, it comes as quite a jolt to discover that they too have been known to make the odd slip between well-rounded phrases. When President Carter paid a visit to Poland the official US interpreter had an off-day.

'I have come to learn your opinions and understand your desires for the future,' the American head of state told his hosts. Or in the words as translated to them, 'I desire the Poles carnally.'

Later in the speech he made a casual reference to his departure from Washington. That was rendered into Polish as 'When I left the United States, never to return.'

Some of the most enduring examples of what one might describe as irregular English occur in signs and notices, frequently in hotels and restaurants it would seem. Out in Baghdad a restaurant was offering an international cuisine that featured: 'Pimps No 1 or Pimps No 2, Shrimps catstails, Escalope Gordon Blue, and Chateaubriani for 3 parsons.'

A hotel in Lausanne warned its residents, 'Meals served in bedroom only in case of decease'. While guests staying in one in Helsinki were invited to take advantage of a novel facility, 'In the hotel restaurant the waitress will give you a bill and you may sign her on the back side.'

Anyone staying at a hotel in Brussels was invited to 'warm the chambermaid in case of fire'.

In a café in Normandy you were cautioned, 'Persons are requested not to occupy seats in this café without consummation.'

And if you happened to stay the night in a certain hotel in Istanbul you'd see the notice advising, 'Ladies are requested not to have children in the cocktail lounge.'

In the context of this book two seminal examples stand out, both interestingly drawn from the English-speaking world. Putting one side of the travel story was a notice in a travel agent's window in Dorking which read, 'Do us a favour and GO AWAY!'

The other was written on the wall of a New York subway station. 'Gloria mundi is sic of the transit,' it read.